T0246272

What thought leaders and investors are saying about *Break the Rules!*

"Stunning! The mindset guide for entrepreneurs who want to stand out from the rest of business leaders and make a difference in their team culture. A must-read!"

—Daniel Marcos
Co-Founder and CEO, Growth Institute

"I've often said that you can't teach a person to be an entrepreneur, but John Mullins's book comes as close as you'll get to doing just that by uncovering the mindsets that lead to entrepreneurial actions. By focusing on these mindsets, Mullins suggests ways to bring out the entrepreneur in many of us."

—Rob Johnson
Visiting Professor, IESE Business School

"The 'entrepreneurial mindset' is an enigma. To the uninitiated it is a mystery how some people just seem to have the knack for recognizing opportunity, attracting talent, and initiating focused, driven collaboration that creates value for customers, and potentially fortunes, for their team, their investors, and themselves. With *Break the Rules!*, John Mullins has decoded the mystery. He pulls back the curtain to reveal six key behaviors that entrepreneurs use to "break the rules" and go where others have feared to tread. With this guide to the entrepreneurial mindset, we have a roadmap that can guide future entrepreneurs and innovators, in big companies as well as startups, to move from insight to action, from idea to impact."

—Jerome Engel
Adjunct Professor (Emeritus),
Haas School of Business, UC Berkeley
Founding Executive Director,
Lester Center for Entrepreneurship and Innovation
Co-Author, *Clusters of Innovation in the Age of Disruption*

"*Break the Rules!* is a highly accessible book that provides crucial insights that will increase the chance of success as an entrepreneur. John Mullins is both a gifted storyteller and an astute observer of the unique attributes and mindsets of those rare individuals who can give birth to major new companies. If you don't have the good fortune of taking one of John's classes, do yourself a favor and read this book."

—Bruce Golden
Partner, Accel

"Research shows that successful entrepreneurs respond differently to events and circumstances than do other decision makers in business. In this insightful and fun-to-read book, best-selling author and business school professor John Mullins uncovers six key elements that constitute the mindset of entrepreneurs, thereby making their unconventional, counterintuitive way of thinking accessible to everyone. With a little reflection and practice you can improve your own entrepreneurial skills!"

—Marc Gruber, PhD
Vice President for Innovation, École Polytechnique Fédérale de
Lausanne (*EPFL*)
Co-Author, *Where to Play*

"It is often said that it isn't about the cards you were dealt or how the game changes while you play it, but rather how you approach it that matters most. In this, his latest book, Professor Mullins accurately captures the biggest weapon an entrepreneur has: their mindset. He outlines the key ingredients of an entrepreneurial mindset in a form that's applicable to current/aspiring entrepreneurs and corporate innovators alike and provides an inspiring set of applied examples to help you, the reader, transform how you approach the inevitable obstacles that will stand in your way."

—Carlos Eduardo Espinal
Managing Partner, Seedcamp
Author, *Fundraising Field Guide*

"*Break the Rules!* does for the entrepreneurial mindset what *Getting to Plan B* and *The Customer-Funded Business* have done for startup founders who need a large dose of reality to succeed at creating sustainable, scalable ventures. Especially noteworthy is the inclusion of both ethical challenges and corporate innovation. The "lessons learned" sections are a treasure trove of invaluable insights gleaned by Mullins's razor-sharp (and always pragmatic) perspectives."

—Lisa Getzler
Executive Director, Baker Institute for Entrepreneurship, Creativity &
Innovation, Lehigh University

"*Break the Rules!* illustrates that changing the world through entrepreneurship requires new ways of thinking and less obvious ways of acting. We are living in a time where we can no longer rely on the big companies to create the future. Everything big starts small, and small is where the magic happens. Mullins reminds us how to create the magic."

—Heidi Neck, PhD
Timmons Professor of Entrepreneurship, Babson College
Chief Education Officer and Co-Founder, Venture Blocks

"As a venture capitalist, I prefer backing mission-driven entrepreneurs who are so passionate about the problem they are solving that it becomes their life's work. But I never thought about segmenting problem-first from product-first. That's a remarkably useful insight. I must admit that I've been blinded by product, especially these days when achieving product-market fit is a celebrated milestone. As always, John's frameworks are actionable, even for an industry veteran like me."

—Hussein Kanji
Partner, Hoxton Ventures

"John Mullins is the easiest-to-understand contrarian in entrepreneurship. Whether it is *Getting to Plan B* or creating *The Customer-Funded Business*, John excels at identifying and teaching us the best and least-traveled paths to success. This volume builds on his approach, providing six ways to think and act like entrepreneurs, and create value for yourself and others. If you read only one John Mullins book, make it this one."

—Jerome Katz, PhD
Brockhaus Chair of Entrepreneurship, Saint Louis University
Author, *Entrepreneurial Small Business*

"Mullins has done it again! In this brilliant book he has captured the essence of the entrepreneurial mindset. His six principles emerge from careful study of scores of successful entrepreneurs across the globe. His practical but counterintuitive advice will drive value in every business."

—Murray Low, PhD
Faculty of Executive Education, Columbia Business School

"What a wonderful read. I truly enjoyed learning about so many interesting cases from all around the world, some well known and highly successful, others less known or ultimately unsuccessful. John Mullins, drawing upon his entrepreneurial and academic experience, has been able to distil important lessons from these cases. Some lessons are intuitive but not always straightforward to implement, others go against conventional wisdom. At the very least, every entrepreneur should carefully consider how these lessons can be used to enhance their own venture."

—Sophie Manigart, PhD
Professor of Corporate Finance and Faculty Dean, Vlerick Business School

"While there is lots of talk about how entrepreneurs *act* differently, the book shows how it all starts with *thinking* differently! The book shows how to think—and act—like an entrepreneur."

—Henning Piezunka, PhD
Associate Professor, INSEAD

"In *Break the Rules! The Six Counter-Conventional Mindsets of Entrepreneurs*, John Mullins brings to bear his decades of experience as an entrepreneur and entrepreneurship educator to distill the six most important mindsets start-up founders and corporate entrepreneurs need to acquire in order to enhance their chances of survival and growth. These mindsets, explained simply and powerfully, emphasize customer centricity, focus, frugality, and proactiveness. The explanation of the mindsets, rightly labeled counter-conventional, is enriched with compelling examples of how entrepreneurs from different countries applied these mindsets to overcome difficulties and build successful organizations."

—S. Ramakrishna Velamuri, PhD
Professor and Dean, Mahindra University School of Management

"John Mullins has done it again! Could not put the book down. Matching takeaways with real-life examples to learn from successes and, equally importantly, failures. Simple, powerful, pragmatic. A must-read."

—Anastasios Economou
Global Chairman, Young Presidents' Organization (YPO)

"In this special book, Mullins has tapped into the essence of entrepreneurship and its power to change people's lives. He translates the entrepreneurial mindset from vague concept to practical guide, showing us how to think and act if we want to launch new things. Through stories and practical examples, he demonstrates how this mindset is not one thing, but six different approaches to making change happen. In the process, he dispels the myths and removes the mystery from what it actually means to *be entrepreneurial*."

—Michael Morris, PhD
University of Notre Dame
Co-Author, *What Do Entrepreneurs Create?*

"John Mullins's experiences as entrepreneur, educator, and author already attest to both the breadth and depth of his true understanding of how entrepreneurship works on the ground and how that can be brought into classrooms. As an entrepreneur and academic who studies mindsets of expert entrepreneurs, I find the six simple rules that John suggests breaking to be delightful, useful, and actionable. From an intellectual perspective, each of these are components of the invaluable "bias for action" that is well attested to in research. In a world in which entrepreneurship education continues to exhibit a misguided bias for analysis and hypothesis testing rather than a quicker move into cocreative action and speedy reaction that characterizes the entrepreneurial mindset, this book serves to get our students and all entrepreneurs 'moving' in the right direction."

—Saras Sarasvathy, PhD
Paul M. Hammaker Professor of Business Administration, The Darden
School, University of Virginia

BREAK
THE
RULES!

CHALLENGE ASSUMPTIONS,
OVERCOME OBSTACLES,
MITIGATE RISK

BREAK
THE
RULES!

The **6** Counter-Conventional
Mindsets of Entrepreneurs

THAT CAN HELP *ANYONE* CHANGE THE WORLD

JOHN MULLINS, PhD

WILEY

Library of Congress Cataloging-in-Publication Data:

Names: Mullins, John W. (John Walker) author.
Title: Break the rules! : the 6 counter-conventional mindsets of
  entrepreneurs that can help anyone change the world / John Mullins.
Description: First edition. | Hoboken, New Jersey: Wiley, [2023] |
  Includes index.
Identifiers: LCCN 2022039111 (print) | LCCN 2022039112 (ebook) | ISBN
  9781394153015 (cloth) | ISBN 9781394153039 (adobe pdf) | ISBN
  9781394153022 (epub)
Subjects: LCSH: Entrepreneurship—Psychological aspects. | Problem solving.
  | Attitude (Psychology) | Organizational effectiveness.
Classification: LCC HB615 .M835 2023 (print) | LCC HB615 (ebook) | DDC
  338/.04—dc23/eng/20220818
LC record available at https://lccn.loc.gov/2022039111
LC ebook record available at https://lccn.loc.gov/2022039112

Cover Design: PAUL MCCARTHY
Cover Image: © GETTY IMAGES | MIRAGE C

SKY10039403_120222

Contents

Acknowledgments

A s I've often said to my students, entrepreneurship played to win is a team sport, not a solo sport, notwithstanding the mythology to the contrary. The same can be said of the creation of a book like the one you now hold in your hands. There are people too numerous to mention—most of them entrepreneurs—from whom I've learned the many lessons that comprise the heart of this book. I thank all of them profusely. Over my three decades as an academic, I've learned above all that wisdom resides mostly outside, not inside, our hallowed halls or our faculty offices or classrooms. Wisdom about what makes entrepreneurs "entrepreneurial" has been out there to be discovered, and the discovery process that's led to this book has been a richly rewarding one.

My thanks must begin with my incredibly able research partner Christina Brant, whose dogged pursuit of every lead and every published article about many of the entrepreneurs and their companies profiled in this book literally made the book possible. Thank you, Christina! Equally important are my past London Business School students and others who collaborated with me in developing the original case studies from which my discovery of these six break-the-rules mindsets arose: Alessandro Ananias and Brian Forde (SubWay Link); Tiffany Putimahtama (MOVE Guides); Darice Gubbins and John Walker (Simon Cohen); David Prinster (Apex Ski Boots); Elizabeth Philp (Pandora); Hicham Sharara (Visual Optical); Shira Conradi (Budgetplaces.com); Ambika Patni and Shreedhar Munshi (The Loot); and Payne Miller and Qusai Kanchwalla (TeamLease).

Without the development of those case studies, the idea for writing this book would have never materialized. And without the incredibly rich learning platform that London Business School has provided to my students and so many others like them from around the world—and to me—we'd all be worse off, for sure. Thank you, LBS, and thanks for the research funding and for our robust intellectual climate, too!

Of course, my thanks go out to the protagonists in these and my many other case studies, the founders, investors, and others who so generously opened their doors, and often their books, so that I might have compelling, real-world teaching materials in my portfolio to enable the next generation of entrepreneurs to learn from the challenges they encountered and their successes and failures of one kind or another: Arnold Correia (SubWay Link); Brynne Kennedy and Steve Black (MOVE Guides); Simon Cohen (Simon Cohen); John Murphy (Apex Ski Boots); Martin Høyer-Hansen, Nikolaj Vejlsgaard, and Per Enevoldsen (Pandora); Aziz Mebarek and Karim Trad (Visual Optical); John Erceg (Budgetplaces.com); Jay Gupta (The Loot); Tristram and Rebecca Mayhew (GoApe!); and Manish Sabharwal and Ashok Reddy (TeamLease). Thank you all.

Thank you to the Young Presidents' Organization and the Entrepreneurs' Organization for trusting me and my London Business School colleagues to develop and deliver impactful annual learning experiences for YPO and EO members since 2003. The learning from which I have benefited has, for me, been exceptional. Most of whatever useful insights and ideas appear in this book are the direct result of conversations with my many YPO and EO friends—whether in their offices or in classroom settings—about their journeys. Any errors in interpreting or understanding the insights, ideas, and the lessons they hold are, of course, mine alone.

The research and the learning, though, is only the start of what makes a book like this possible. The encouragement of the wonderful Eloise Cook and former *Business Horizons* editor Jeffery McMullen (who published my earlier and much more succinct journal-article-length treatment of these ideas) convinced me that the effort to turn my earlier observations into a book were going to be worth the time and effort. Thank you, Eloise and Jeff.

Wiley's Richard Narramore was instrumental in helping me envision who the audience for this book might be. His belief that the six mindsets hold promise for pretty much any businessperson—not just entrepreneurs—has shaped the book in many ways. Thanks, Richard, for your insights and your focus on the importance of identifying and articulating the benefits that this book might deliver.

As was the case in publishing my first Wiley book, *The Customer-Funded Business*, the entire Wiley team has been a joy to work with. Kim Wimpsett, my developmental editor, brought keen insights to much of the prose and, in particular, to the titles and subtitles we've given each chapter. Details like these matter. Thank you, Kim! The work of the Straive design team and Paul McCarthy's work on the book's cover were superb. I love the broken pencil, Paul! Last but not least, managing editor Debbie Schindlar and the incredibly well-organized Jessica Filippo helped us all keep the trains running on time! Thanks to all of you and your colleagues at Wiley!

Finally, my heartfelt thanks go to my family. My parents, the late Jack and Alice Mullins, who instilled in me from an early age a love of learning and of writing, too. My wife Donna, whose love and patience have sustained our relationship for nearly 50 years. Every time I embark on writing a book, Donna worries that she will see "a lot of the back of my head" as I focus for months on end with bringing a book like this one into being. And she was right—again! Though Donna might like me to slow down just a little, at least sometime soon, the words "slow" and "stop" just don't seem to be part of my lexicon. The fact that

I love writing and I love my work—as much as I love Colorado's great outdoors and London's incredible vitality and cultural diversity—makes me a fortunate person, indeed, sometimes to Donna's chagrin. Thank you, Donna, for sharing with me all the adventures we've had together over so many years, book-writing among them.

I'll close by thanking all the entrepreneurs whose creative and tireless efforts, often against long odds, have made our world a better place to live, to work, and to play. It is they who create the vast majority of the net new jobs around the world. It is they who provide opportunities for their employees to work, learn, and grow—and perhaps adopt their own entrepreneurial mind-sets, too. It's they, more than anyone else, in my view, who hold the key to our collective future. I hope you, my readers, will bring *your* entrepreneurial talent and energy—and your new entrepreneurial mindset—to the party and join them!

John Mullins
Summer 2022
www.johnwmullins.com
www.break-the-rules.net

Preface: Why This Book?

These days, it seems, just about everybody wants to be an entrepreneur or part of a fast-growing entrepreneurial venture. Most large companies say they want to be more entrepreneurial, too, though most don't like the risk and uncertainty that comes with the territory. Sadly, however, most entrepreneurial ventures fail—some sooner, some later—so the entrepreneurial path, whether for those who lead the journey or those who participate therein, is typically rocky at best.

With that reality in mind, a couple of years ago, I was taking stock of what I'd learned over my many years of both having been an entrepreneur—with a win, a draw, and a loss to my name—and having studied entrepreneurs of all shapes,

> **Entrepreneurs and the counter-conventional mindsets they embrace are different from most other businesspeople in some fundamental ways—six ways, as it turns out.**

sizes, and aspirations during this, my second career as a business school professor. A picture—an epiphany, perhaps—emerged: Entrepreneurs are different from the rest of their peers in the business world. I'd seen it. I'd heard it. I'd felt it. You may know it to be true, too. Duh! Entrepreneurs and the counter-conventional mindsets they embrace are different from most other businesspeople in some fundamental ways—six ways, as it turns out. But, so what? Why might my discovery be of interest to a reader like you?

My Epiphany: It's Your Mindset That Can Take You Where You Want to Go

From my ringside seat, I've observed closely how many of the world's most successful entrepreneurs think and act. How they take in information and what they do with it. How they respond to circumstances that come their way. In short, I've observed that what's different about successful entrepreneurs is not their drive, as most are no more or no less driven than many leaders in the corporate world are. It's not their personalities, as they are all as different as you are from me. It's not their willingness to take risk, because what the good ones do is find ways to offload the ever-present risk onto others or mitigate it. They manage risk. They don't take risk, at least not willingly.

So, what's the difference? It's their *mindsets* that cause entrepreneurs to think and act fundamentally differently from many of their peers in large, well-established businesses. Moreover, these mindsets fly in the face of much of what we teach—and have taught for decades—in business schools. They fly in the face of what we have come to accept as near-universal truths about how business works. They fly in the face of what most people think one should do to lead and manage a successful business. In short, they break the conventional rules.

> **These mindsets fly in the face of much of what we teach—and have taught for decades—in business schools.**

Thus, in this book, you'll read about these counter-conventional, break-the-rules mindsets, six of them, to be exact. They will be brought to life by the stories of well-known and iconic entrepreneurs like Tesla's Elon Musk, Bharti AirTel's Sunil Bharti Mittal, Amazon's Jeff Bezos, and others. They'll also be brought to life, perhaps surprisingly, by the stories of inspiring entrepreneurs who are much like you. Men and women who have created and led unsung, little-known entrepreneurial ventures to sometimes modest, sometimes astonishing levels of success. Even people who have broken the conventional rules to get things done inside large established businesses like Nestlé.

A book was needed to bring the mindsets they so viscerally demonstrate to life so you, too, can put their lessons into your entrepreneurial persona, so the world can benefit from what you create and deliver. With your new mindset in hand, you'll be well prepared to embark on or ramp up an entrepreneurial journey to wherever you'd like to go, whether your journey begins in a co-working space, in your kitchen or garage, or deep inside an established organization!

Making *Their* Mindsets *Yours*

I'll introduce the book in Chapter 1, where I'll tell one such story and provide an overview of the six counter-conventional, break-the-rules mindsets that characterize some of yesterday's, today's, and I expect tomorrow's most inspiring entrepreneurs. In Chapters 2 through 7, I'll then dig deeply into each of the six mindsets, one chapter and one mindset at a time, drawing from these remarkable case studies the lessons that readers like you can learn and put into practice.

Happily, in my work with thousands of entrepreneurs from all over the world, I've discovered that the six mindsets can be **❝Breaking the conventional rules is not rocket science. It's an attitude. A mindset.❞** taught, and, even better, they can be learned and applied in business and other organizational settings of all sizes and kinds. Breaking the conventional rules is not rocket science. It's an attitude. A mindset. It's what's enabled so many entrepreneurs to transform the way we live, work, and play today. Their mindsets—and *yours*—hold the key that can sometimes make the impossible possible.

Who Should Read This Book?

If you are someone who wants to start or grow your own entrepreneurial venture or work in a fast-growing company, one that's going to make the world just a bit better in one way or another, this book is for you.

Similarly, if you're the leader of a larger and more established, and perhaps slower-growing, business and you're trying to find people who are—or teach people to be—more "entrepreneurial" than the sometimes set-in-their-ways employees who make change so difficult to carry out in organizations like yours, this book is for you, too.

As observer Bill Joy noted nearly two decades ago, in describing what was happening in large companies at that time in a short but profound op-ed piece in *Fortune* magazine, "Innovation is happening everywhere. But mostly elsewhere."[1]

So, let me be clear. Who is this book for?

- Aspiring entrepreneurs of any age and any level of business experience who are considering setting forth on an entrepreneurial journey into what is always the unknown. I don't have to tell you that you'll face long odds. This book will help you confront them.
- Those already walking the entrepreneurial path with dreams of scaling up. The sad reality is that most start-ups remain small forever. They simply don't scale, for one reason or another. This book's insights will help *you* be among those whose businesses do.
- Anyone else in business, anywhere, who wants to make their part of the business—or all of it, if you're its leader—more "entrepreneurial." And, in so doing, change the world, or at least your small part of it.

Why John Mullins?

For more than 30 years, I've had the good fortune to rigorously study what makes entrepreneurs tick and their ventures thrive—or fail. I've done this in three ways, each of which has served as an important source of the insights into entrepreneurs and their mindsets that this book delivers.

The first way is by having researched and written three trade books, each chock-full of captivating and insightful case studies, from which I've learned so much. Each of those books focused on one crucial aspect of the entrepreneurial journey: assessing opportunities, so you pursue an attractive one and don't waste your time on the pursuit of a no-hoper (*The New Business Road Test*); figuring out a business model that will actually work (*Getting to Plan B*); and finding a way to finance your venture without selling your soul—and your freedom and control—to business angels or venture capital investors (*The Customer-Funded Business*). These three books, taken together, have set the stage for the insights in this one.

The second source of my "entrepreneurs are different" epiphany and the insights that comprise it, and the one to which I've devoted most of my research and writing time, is the case studies I've developed on more than 50 entrepreneurial companies and their founders. The process of developing all these case studies has afforded me an intimate ringside seat into what's driven their entrepreneurial journeys—some phenomenally successful, others less so.

> **The process of developing all these case studies has afforded me an intimate ringside seat.**

The third source, and perhaps the richest, is the opportunity to have led engaging case discussions with thousands of highly motivated, high-powered entrepreneurs over the past 20 years. Thanks to my role as an entrepreneurship professor at one of the world's top business schools, I've been privileged to develop and deliver executive education programs for members of the Young Presidents' Organization (YPO) and the Entrepreneurs' Organization (EO) annually since 2003.

The learning that goes on within such learning communities—whether peer to peer, professor to participants, or, most importantly, in the creation of this book, participants to professor—is a highlight of my work, year after year. This book would not exist without the knowledge I've gained from and about so many YPOers and EOers. It's their embodiment of these six counter-conventional, break-the-rules mindsets that we can thank for whatever lessons you take away from this book.

Off You Go!

If you are among those who are eager to be a leader and change maker, whether in a new venture of your own choosing, in a fast-growing start-up that looks like it might be on a glide path to the moon, or in a much larger enterprise that's seeking to become more entrepreneurial, adopting any of these six mindsets into who *you* are will be well worth your time and effort. I promise. Are you intrigued? Turn the page and get started on breaking the rules!

JWM, Summer 2022

1

It's Time to Break the Rules: Challenge Assumptions, Overcome Obstacles, Mitigate Risk

A re you ready to adopt your own entrepreneurial mindset? Let's dive right in. Buckle your seatbelt, because here we go!

A $1.5 Billion Story That Begins with "No"[1]

It was 1984, and Lynda Weinman had just bought a Macintosh computer. Thanks to its user-friendly interface, Weinman, with the occasional help of Mac user group meetings, taught herself how to use it. "I was doggedly persistent and stubborn about wanting to learn it. You could just try everything and you're not going to break it," she remembers.[2] Before long, she was getting hired to do contract work for Hollywood animators, including working directly with film director William Shatner, where she worked on animations for the movie *Star Trek V: The Last Frontier.* What she didn't yet know how to do, she figured out.

By the early 1990s, she found herself teaching graphic arts at the Art Center College of Design in Pasadena, California, where she was teaching students how to use tools like the then-new-fangled Photoshop, Illustrator, and other computer graphics software. She was looking for a web design book she could assign to her students. Searching the bookstore, she grew more and more frustrated. She found only complicated technical guides that were impossible for the average person to understand. "I remember thinking, maybe this book doesn't exist yet," she says. "I went home from the bookstore and wrote the book proposal."[3] Alas, the proposal was rejected.

"No" Is an Answer Waiting to Be Turned into "Yes"

Ever-persistent, as was her style, Weinman convinced a magazine publisher to let her publish her book chapters as a series of monthly columns. While researching one of the chapters, she came across a website called debbie.com, which was compiling all the Debbies on the Internet, consisting of only about 20 Debbies at the time! "I wonder if lynda.com is available," she asked herself. It was, and for $35 she bought it, using it as her sandbox to teach herself web design and as a place where she could gather and post resources to which she could refer her students.

Eventually, she found a publisher, a division of Macmillan, to publish her first book, *Designing Web Graphics*, in 1996. "It's a book on web design, but no one has a website! They did not have a website!" she exclaimed. "Art Center doesn't! But I do!"[4] The book quickly became the top-selling web design book in the world. The lynda.com website, mentioned therein, got more and more popular, and before long it was ranked among the top 100 websites in the world. Weinman began getting teaching and speaking gigs about web design anywhere and everywhere.

The Second "No"

With a highly successful first book plus a second one with her husband Bruce Heavin also in print, the couple decided to quit their day jobs and move to Ojai, an idyllic resort town not far north of Los Angeles.[5] Heavin had an idea. "If they'll pay for you to teach a workshop in Peoria, Illinois, why wouldn't they pay for you to have a workshop in Ojai, California, and why don't we produce our own workshops?"[6] But there was nowhere they could find to teach. Another "No." Fortuitously, they were able to convince a local school to let them use its computer lab during spring break. In 1996, they placed an ad on lynda.com. The workshop sold out, with one of the attendees coming from as far away as Vienna, Austria!

In 1998, the couple opened a school, the Ojai Digital Arts Center, and started hiring other teachers that Weinman knew from the speaking circuit. "We had so many customers, we were turning them away," she says.[7] In the school's first year in business, it did $1.7 million in revenue, with payment made weeks or months in advance. Even leading companies like Adobe and Martha Stewart were sending their employees.

> **In the school's first year in business, it did $1.7 million in revenue, with payment made weeks or months in advance.**

The Third "No"

Weinman was eager to publish more books on additional topics in her burgeoning field. But her publisher didn't see eye to eye with her for some of them. She turned to video, using the main recording and playback medium of that time, VHS tapes. Soon, checks were arriving in their post office box, with the training tapes shipped out the same way. It was a simple mail order business. The business grew, and by 2001, annual revenue hit $3.7 million.[8]

Disaster Strikes, Opportunity Beckons

The attacks on New York City's Twin Towers on September 11, 2001, caused air travel to dry up overnight. "No one wanted to

❝"There's only so much you can do with a couple of kids in a shipping room."❞ come to Ojai, California, for a training class," Weinman recalls.[9] At the same time, the dot-com boom of the late 1990s was turning to dust. "People who had been paying to come to our workshops had been doing it with funny money. We were very worried that we were going to go out of business." Staff was cut from 35 to 9 to keep the business afloat. Heavin came up with another idea. "There's only so much you can do with a couple of kids in a shipping room."[10] He wanted to start selling their videos online.

They started with 24 courses in 2002, the same things they'd been teaching and writing about. "We were way too early," recalls Weinman. The Internet was dial-up in those days, and bandwidth was limited. By the end of the first year, they had only 1,000 customers paying $25 per month for a subscription that provided access to all their titles. Worse, subscriptions were cannibalizing the sale of the stand-alone videos, which were being sold at $150 each.

Nonetheless, sales grew and within less than five years, the company was back to its pre-2001 revenue level. They stopped in-person classes. Stopped writing books. No more DVDs. They went all-in on the online idea. As it turned out, people everywhere who taught Photoshop and web design were using Weinman's courses and bringing them into their schools and into their companies. Says Heavin, "We'd be installed in all of Apple, all of Adobe, all of Microsoft, all of Google. And the employees were starting to demand that companies bring it in. It was just a word-of-mouth thing."[11]

The Rest of the Story

In 2007, having passed the 100,000-subscriber milestone, they brought in an outside CEO, Eric Robison. "We were fumbling with success," says Heavin. "Here I am an art student, and Lynda is a teacher. We had no business background."[12] Revenue had hit $10 million and California's venture capital community had noticed. The phone was ringing off the hook.

As the new team took shape, they stepped on the gas. Sales reached $100 million in 2012. In 2013, somewhat reluctantly, the couple finally took outside investment. The business grew even faster and in 2015, LinkedIn made an unsolicited offer to buy the business. LinkedIn wanted to broaden its business from helping its users with "How to get a job" and add "How to get trained." LinkedIn paid $1.5 billion for the business, which they subsequently rebranded as LinkedIn Learning. The business that Weinman and Heavin had lovingly nurtured for nearly 20 years had made its mark!

Why the Success?

"Lynda.com was ed tech before ed tech was cool," said Betsy Corcoran, chief executive of EdSurge, an information resource on educational technology.[13] "It's one of those overnight success stories that wasn't overnight at all," said Raymond Pirouz, formerly Director of Marketing at lynda.com.[14] Weinman explains:

> I'd like to believe that we were doing something differently. I think we had a teaching pedagogy that other training companies did not use. It was about making the information very approachable, breaking things into bits. And it's freedom. You're not in a classroom; you're not getting a grade. It's really tapping into this beautiful learning philosophy that I've been living my entire life that is just curiosity. Learn interesting things. Learn things that give you joy.[15]

But there was much more to this remarkable success story than meets Weinman's self-effacing eye.

Weinman's Counter-Conventional, Break-the-Rules Mindset

Arguably, Weinman changed the world for many of the more than 4 million students who took one or more of lynda.com's online courses. New skills. New passions. New jobs. New careers. Lynda Weinman is the poster child, the exemplar entrepreneur, perhaps, whose journey foretells the lessons I'm about to impart in this book. Turning "no" into "yes" three times only scratches the surface.

> **Though Weinman probably didn't know it at the time, she and Heavin consciously or unconsciously broke many of the rules that define how business is conventionally done.**

Though Weinman probably didn't know it at the time, she and Heavin consciously or unconsciously broke many of the rules that define how business is conventionally done. What she didn't yet know how to do, like graphically build the hull of the Starship Enterprise, she figured out—her *prior competencies* or lack thereof be damned. She was *problem*-focused (on her students' learning) and relaxed about what sort of *product*—a college class, a book or magazine article, a video, or whatever—could best deliver a compelling solution. She chose to serve an extremely *narrow target market* at the outset—Apple Macintosh users who wanted to learn graphic arts skills. She always asked for *payment up front*—a publisher's advance for her books, payment in advance for her courses. She and Heavin *borrowed* a high school computer lab to test their idea of running workshops in Ojai.

As we'll see in Chapters 2 through 6, these practices run counter to the spoken or unspoken rules that most large companies typically follow. And they run counter to some of what's taught in business schools like mine. In my view, it was Weinman's innate entrepreneurial mindset, as much as her superb pedagogy, that made her journey so successful. Fortunately for you, you don't have to have been born with the six break-the-rules elements of an entrepreneurial mindset.

You can learn them and apply them. Entrepreneurs are made, at least most of the time, not born.

So What's a Mindset?

What, you might ask, do I mean by *mindset?* As best-selling author and social psychologist Carol Dweck puts it, a mindset is a self-perception or "self-theory" that people hold about themselves.[16] More particularly, mindsets are the "collection of beliefs and thoughts that make up the mental attitude, inclination,

> **Most successful entrepreneurs interpret and respond differently to events, circumstances, and situations than do their more conventionally minded business peers.**

habit or disposition that predetermines a person's interpretations and responses to events, circumstances and situations."[17] More than two decades of my research has taught me that most successful entrepreneurs interpret and respond differently to events, circumstances, and situations than do their more conventionally minded business peers.

In the remainder of this book, you'll read 19 inspiring (or occasionally discomforting) case studies of world-class entrepreneurs—some whose familiar names you'll find in the business press regularly, and others who you'll hear about for the first time in these pages. These case studies will vividly bring to life the six break-the-rules, counter-conventional mindsets of entrepreneurs (see Figure 1.1).

- **"Yes, we can!":** When asked by a prospective customer whether they can do something that's entirely new and unfamiliar and falls outside their current competencies, entrepreneurs say "Yes, we can!" Then they figure out how!
- **Problem-first, not product-first, logic:** Entrepreneurs know that if they solve genuine customer problems, their

FIGURE 1.1   The six counter-conventional mindsets

businesses will thrive! As one prominent venture capital investor famously remarked, "It's very simple. Nobody will pay you to solve a non-problem."[18]

- **Think narrow, not broad:** Big companies want to serve big markets: "It won't move the needle," they say when markets are small. But once success is established in a tiny market, entrepreneurs know, a foundation is in place to enable their businesses to grow from there.

- **Ask for the cash, ride the float:** By getting customers to pay in advance, and by paying their suppliers afterwards, entrepreneurs "ride the float" and put that cash into growing their businesses.

- **Beg, borrow, but don't steal:** Borrowing the resources you need to start something new beats investing in those resources, especially as the outcomes of almost anything new are highly uncertain.

- **Instead of asking permission, beg forgiveness later:** Getting new things done in established companies typically requires permission, sometimes from higher-ups in the organization, sometimes from company lawyers, sometimes from regulators or others. When the legal or regulatory landscape is ambiguous or uncertain, entrepreneurs simply plow ahead and deal with any necessary regulatory issues later, begging forgiveness if necessary.

Did Weinman run her business with an entrepreneurial mindset? Did she break the conventional rules? Time after time! So, too, can *you*!

Breaking the Rules

Best-selling author Francesca Gino says it simply, in her 2018 book, *Rebel Talent: Why It Pays to Break the Rules at Work and in Life*: "Most businesses are all about following the rules, not breaking them."[19] But she also observes that breaking the rules is associated with innovation. It's about courage. About bringing about positive change. About making the world a better place. Most entrepreneurs I know are all about changing the world. Sometimes in a big way; think Elon Musk. Sometimes in their small corner of the world or for some small audience; think Lynda Weinman at the outset of her journey.

This book is all about breaking the conventional rules that are so dearly held in most big companies, and in business schools, too. It's about teaching you how to adopt a counter-conventional mindset so you, too, can put it to use in your endeavors. Whether you're about to embark—or you've already embarked—on an entrepreneurial journey; whether you're working deep in the bowels of a big company that needs to get out of its slow-growth rut—or you're a leader hoping to drag your people kicking and screaming into more counter-conventional thinking and acting; or even if you're a student thinking about starting your business or working for a start-up, this book and these six mindsets are for you!

Why Break the Rules Now?

As I write in mid-2022, the world is replete with daunting challenges: pervasive economic and social inequality the world over; war in Europe; a warming planet; political discord and dysfunction seemingly everywhere. And more. Regardless of whether we like it or not, the conventional rules and conventional behavior seem not to be making much progress. But entrepreneurs—and sometimes those working in established companies, too—can and often do make a difference.

> **If you have an idea about how to make your corner of the world a better place—in a small way or large—now is the time.**

As we'll see in Chapter 4, Elon Musk has almost single-handedly made electric vehicles relevant, against long odds. As we'll see in Chapter 6, Sunil Bharti Mittal brought mobile phones to rural India—profitably! As we'll see in Chapter 7, Manish Sabharwal and Ashok Reddy have brought more than 3 million mostly young people into the Indian workforce. If you have an idea about how to make your corner of the world a better place—in a small way or large—*now* is the time. And a key ingredient in making that happen—*your* entrepreneurial mindset—is here in the book you now hold in your hands.

What Lies Ahead

In this Chapter 1, through Lynda Weinman's case study, I've brought to life what it means to be an accomplished entrepreneur—yesterday, today, and tomorrow—and what makes her tick. I've explained what I mean by *mindset* and briefly overviewed the six mindsets that comprise a "mindset menu" from which you can choose those you wish to make your own.

And I've argued for the importance of breaking the conventional rules—and breaking them now.

In Chapters 2 through 7, the beating heart of the book, I'll dig deeply into each of the six counter-conventional mindsets, one chapter for each. You'll get inspiring case studies of entrepreneurs—some of them inside big companies, perhaps to your surprise—who bring these mindsets to life. In each of these chapters you'll also get the story of a not-so-inspiring failure. Isn't failure often the best teacher? As some say in Silicon Valley, failure is an education on somebody else's dollar! But there's more. In each of these six core chapters, I draw lessons you can take away from the case studies therein, together with steps *you* can take now to make that chapter's mindset your own.

Then, to tie things together, in Chapter 8 I'll examine how best to get started on your journey toward making these mind-sets yours, depending on who you are and where you sit:

- An aspiring entrepreneur
- Someone already traveling an entrepreneurial path
- Anyone in business elsewhere, whether you're the leader of that business or someone doing your best to make things happen from deep inside
- Or even a student pondering an entrepreneurial career

Finally, I'll address four key obstacles that will undoubtedly stand in your way, and how to overcome them. And I'll wish you *Bon voyage!*

What This Book Is Not

This book, and I say this emphatically, is *not* about breaking the law, a theme I'll explore in some depth in Chapter 7. It's not about how to discover a promising entrepreneurial opportunity or how to get a job in a fast-growing entrepreneurial venture, though it may well help you succeed in either role. It's not about how to start a new venture, or grow an existing one, either, although adopting one or more of the six mindsets will surely help you make progress in either of those endeavors. It's not about planning, or strategy, or financing, or exits, though it will probably illuminate those things, too. Perhaps most importantly, it's not for entrepreneurs alone for, as you'll see, the six mindsets are occasionally found in very large and well-established companies, too.

The Book in a Nutshell

Reading this book from cover to cover will equip you with a counter-conventional, break-the-rules mindset to enable you to challenge assumptions, overcome obstacles, and mitigate risk. Better yet, I hope it will inspire you to take on and address the kinds of meaningful challenges that only entrepreneurs dare to take on. As the famous anthropologist Margaret Mead noted long ago, "Never doubt that a small group of thoughtful, committed citizens can change the world; indeed, it's the only thing that ever has."[20] Are you ready to join them? Read on!

2

When You're Tempted to Say No, Instead Say "Yes, We Can!": Then Figure Out How

For more than four decades, the widely accepted wisdom in the world of business has been that the most successful companies are those that pursue opportunities for which the necessary competencies are already in hand. Tom Peters and Bob Waterman, in their classic 1982 book *In Search of Excellence*, argued that businesses should "stick to their knitting," staying true to the business they know, rather than diversifying beyond what they're good at.[1]

Similarly, strategy gurus C. K. Prahalad and Gary Hamel built their academic careers on the back of their classic 1990 article that argued that what good companies should do is clarify their core competencies and then build upon and enhance them.[2] Honda's core competencies in engines and power trains, for example, have provided the underlying basis for business units that manufacture products as diverse as motorcycles, automobiles, lawn mowers, and more. 3M's core competencies in coatings, substrates, and adhesives have enabled it to develop an ever-expanding product line that combines these competencies in various ways.

Makes good sense, right? Further support for this view comes from the waves of spin-offs and divestments that inevitably follow periods during which some businesses have strayed from their knitting and built highly diverse conglomerates, as they're called. General Electric, which had diversified from its late nineteenth-century roots in Thomas Edison's invention of the electric light bulb, became the most valuable company in the world by the 1990s. GE was operating an assortment of mostly unrelated businesses that included home appliances, jet engines, electrical power systems, home and automobile financing, among many others.

Alas, a severe and persistent downturn in GE's financial performance led it to sell off numerous businesses, including its finance business, the legacy light-bulb business, oil and gas services, home appliances, and aircraft leasing. In 2021, GE announced that it would go further and break its remaining operations into three separate companies. "When conglomerates break apart into more focused companies," *Knowledge at Wharton* reports, "those offspring tend to post higher returns and have better operational performance because they devote all their attention and resources to a single core competence."[3]

Many entrepreneurs beg to differ: Whether it gets its start in a garage, at a kitchen table, or deep inside an established business, the entrepreneurial journey is a highly uncertain one, and there's often a surprise along the path. Perhaps a customer asks for something other than what the business has been offering to date. Perhaps the entrepreneur spots an opportunity that appears more attractive than the one currently being pursued. Or perhaps the entrepreneur whiffs the scent of change in the air and detects a potentially existential threat to her business.

Indeed, at a 2008 roundtable meeting of founders of the early-stage companies backed by the storied venture capital firm Kleiner, Perkins, Caufield and Byers, KPCB partner Randy Komisar posed a question: "Which companies had abandoned their original business plans for a Plan B or beyond?" Two-thirds of the hands went up. Remarkably, perhaps, on average these founders had done three restarts each! The premise on which they had pitched for and won KPCB's capital had not panned out.[4]

Thus, for many entrepreneurs, sticking to their knitting simply isn't part of their mindset. It's a rule they simply don't accept. Instead, their mantra is, "Yes, we can!" What about competencies, Peters and Waterman might ask? "We'll find them," they reply. Straying from one's knitting, and moving outside one's current set of core competencies? "Yes, we can!" If the current path looks like it's not going to take them where they want to go, it's time to set out on a new path, they figure. Competencies and the conventional rules be damned.

> **For many entrepreneurs, sticking to their knitting simply isn't part of their mindset. It's a rule they simply don't accept.**

What's ahead in Chapter 2: In this chapter, we'll first examine the case study of Jeff Bezos's historic and counter-conventional decision at Amazon to build a hardware product that would become the Kindle. That was definitely not a project for which his company had the competencies in hand. But a decade later, Amazon was selling a whopping 40 percent of all new books in the United States and two thirds of all e-books.[5] We'll then join Brazilian entrepreneur Arnold Correia on a journey that saw him completely reinvent his business three times and take his company, Atmo Digital, into a leadership position in Brazil's out-of-home media industry.

In both these examples, we'll see how the customer—indeed, in Amazon's case, *obsession* with the customer—played a central role, not only in the decision to stray from their prior knitting but in the approaches these entrepreneurs developed to reach their goals.

But straying from one's knitting doesn't always pan out, of course. Sadly, we'll also learn some sobering lessons from MOVE Guides, a VC-backed start-up in London. Brynne Kennedy's efforts to transform the business from one that provided software-enabled support for the lump-sum moves of junior employees making international corporate relocations into white-glove tailored support for relocating senior executives did not end well. Was it a lack of competencies that led to this failure? Or was it something else? We'll see.

We'll then close the chapter by examining the lessons that these case studies deliver, and we'll address some tangible steps you can take now to make "Yes, we can!" a centerpiece of *your* entrepreneurial mindset. Read on!

The Reshaping of Amazon[6]

It was January 2004. Steve Kessel had risen through the ranks at Amazon to become VP of its worldwide media retailing business, comprising books, music, and video. Amazon founder and CEO Jeff Bezos asked Kessel to step out of that role, in which he was responsible for a whopping 77 percent of Amazon's global revenue,[7] and step into a newly created role, reporting directly to Bezos.

Bezos had decided that Amazon was standing at an important crossroads and it was time to act. Apple had launched the iPod in 2001, which was selling like hotcakes. But Steve Jobs wanted to sell the music, too. In April 2003, Apple had introduced the iTunes store. After selling more than a million downloads on its first day, it went on to sell more than 7.5 million tunes by July 2003.[8] *Time* magazine had named the iTunes store the Coolest Invention of 2003. Sales of Amazon's music CDs were slumping in favor of digital downloads, one tune at a time. "Would books be next?" Bezos wondered.

Kessel's Challenge

Bezos didn't specify *what* was to be done. That would be Kessel's job to figure out, working hand-in hand with Bezos. But Bezos did make two critical *who* (Kessel would take the lead) and *how* decisions. The effort would be run by an entirely new and autonomous organization separate from the existing retail business, despite the fact that the digital media to be sold would presumably be sourced from the same set of publishers that Amazon's current book, music, and video business relied on.

Bill Carr, whom Kessel appointed to run the business side of the new effort alongside an engineering lead, recalls Bezos's logic. "Jeff felt that if we tried to manage digital media as a part of the physical media business, it would never be a priority. The bigger business carried the company after all, and it would always get the most attention."[9] Bezos was adamant. "If you are running both businesses, you will never go after the digital opportunity with tenacity."[10]

"Yes, We Can!"

It quickly became apparent that the core competencies on which Amazon's retail business had been built were of little value in building a digital business. Amazon was mainly an aggregator and distributor of books and music and video discs—all small, lightweight, inexpensive to ship, and unlikely to be damaged in shipment—with the largest assortment found anywhere. It had built a network of highly efficient distribution centres strategically located to integrate with the inbound and outbound logistics of FedEx, UPS, and the United States Postal Service and their counterparts overseas.

❝Kessel and Bezos saw that Amazon's competitive advantage in the distribution business—its vast selection, low prices, and quick delivery—simply would not apply in a new digital business.❞

As a result, its cost structure was far lower than those of its principal competitors, traditional bricks-and-mortar bookstores and retailers of music CDs and video DVDs. Thus Amazon could profitably sell books, music, and videos at far lower prices. Its competitive positioning *vis-à-vis* the bricks-and-mortar competitors appeared unassailable. But Kessel and Bezos saw that Amazon's competitive advantage in the distribution business—its vast selection, low prices, and quick delivery—simply would not apply in a new digital business in which there was nothing physical to warehouse or ship!

To Bezos, that meant that Amazon would have to venture into one end or the other of the value chain, just as Apple was doing with its iTunes and iPod. Content creation or content consumption: which would it be? But Amazon had developed no competencies in either arena. Though no one at Amazon knew anything whatsoever about building hardware, Bezos and Kessel decided that the place to start was at the consumption end of the chain: they would create a better e-reader.

To those who wondered how Amazon could pull off such a brazen move, Kessel reminded his colleagues that typical companies that wanted to grow would consider their existing capabilities and ask, "What can we do next with our skill set?"[11] Amazon's approach, however, as embodied in the first of its core leadership principles, was to start with the customer and "work backwards" and to "obsess over customers."[12] If Amazon's future customers wanted digital delivery, that's what Amazon would provide. If the company lacked the requisite skills, it would have to build or acquire them. There was no other way. What about the rule that one's company should build on its existing core competencies? Easy. Break it!

But How?

To Kessel, building or acquiring new competencies meant one thing: hiring the right team. In September 2004, he hired Gregg Zehr, a long-time hardware industry veteran who had been VP of hardware engineering at Palm Computing and Apple. The hardware talent pool in Silicon Valley was much deeper than that in Seattle, so Zehr set up the hardware operation there, calling it Lab126 (the 1 and the 26 stood for the letters A and Z). The name, a subtle reminder of Bezos's vision to offer any book ever published, from A to Z, was intended to aid Zehr in attracting the best and brightest engineering talent in Silicon Valley. Carr recalls what drove the decision. "We needed talent, and Silicon Valley was where the talent was."[13] Hardware leadership, done.

Building a hardware device was only part of the challenge Kessel faced, of course. He hired other leaders to develop the necessary product and cloud software teams and before long there was a 150-person team of engineers and product managers on board. Additionally, Amazon identified a small 10-person company, Mobipocket, in France that had built software for reading books on PCs and mobile devices. Amazon acquired the company and its team and made them responsible for developing the software for what would soon be the Kindle e-reader.

Creating the Kindle

Bezos set for the team an audacious goal: "improving on an invention that had withstood the test of time, over 500 years, without much change: the book."[14] It was Bezos's view that the customer experience demanded that the e-reader would "get out of the way" so the reader could connect directly with the content. Earlier in his days with Apple, Zehr had worked with a global design firm, Pentagram. Kessel knew that getting the product design right would permit the kind of user experience that Bezos wanted. Pentagram was hired.

Pentagram's designers began studying the actual physics of reading. How do people hold a book? How do they turn the pages? The design team themselves read books on other e-readers from Sony and others and on personal digital assistants (PDAs). "We were pushing for the subconscious qualities that made it feel like you are reading a book," recalled Tom Hobbs, one of Pentagram's designers.[15]

The team wanted to remove every bit of complexity possible and make the device inconspicuous. Bezos shared their view but wanted the device to have a keyboard so users could search for book titles and make annotations if they wished. Bezos also insisted upon wireless connectivity. "Here's my scenario," he told the Pentagram team. "I'm going to the airport. I need a book to read. I want to enter it into the device and download it right there from my car."[16]

"But you can't do that," Hobbs replied, having been unable to figure out how the economics of a wireless connection would work and be paid for. "I'll decide what I can do," replied Bezos. "I'll figure this out and it is not going to be a business model you understand. You are the designers; I want you to design this and I'll think about the business model."[17]

E-books, Too

Bezos's goal was to have 100,000 titles available at launch, including at least 90 percent of the *New York Times* bestsellers. But by 2006 the publishers had only digitized 20,000 titles and most were unhappy with e-books' progress. Their digital sales remained infinitesimal. Another Amazon newcomer, Jeff Steele, a former Microsoft product manager, was charged, alongside another Amazon veteran, with getting US publishers on board. "I described my job as dragging publishers kicking and screaming into the 21st century," he recalled.[18]

Amazon, an increasingly important retailer of physical books, had clout and was not afraid to use it. Randy Miller was responsible for publisher relations in Europe. Miller ranked all the European publishers by their Amazon sales and profit margins. He and his team then persuaded the lagging vendors to give Amazon what it wanted, brazenly using a threat of decreased promotions on the Amazon site.

"I did everything I could to screw with their performance," Miller noted.[19] He raised some books' pricing to list price. He took others out of Amazon's recommendation engine. He promoted competing titles. Amazon was finally learning the ruthless, age-old and brutally effective tricks of the retail trade that Walmart and others had raised to a fine art. Amazon was going to get what it wanted from the publishers—more titles digitized, and better terms, too— one way or another. Thanks to Miller's team's effort in Europe and Steele's progress in North America, the publishers slowly began to come around.

> **Amazon was finally learning the ruthless, age-old and brutally effective tricks of the retail trade that Walmart and others had raised to a fine art.**

The Kindle Launch and Relaunch

Kessel had carefully studied the launches of other new consumer electronic products, including the iPod. He placed an order for 25,000 units with Kindle's Asian suppliers. On November 19, 2007, the Kindle launched. In five-and-a-half hours, the Kindle was sold out! Unfortunately, due to the many delays in getting the hardware right and getting publishers on board, it turned out that one supplier had discontinued a key component in the wireless module. It was nearly a year before Amazon was able to get Kindle back in stock. On October 24, 2008, US TV star Oprah Winfrey devoted an entire episode of her show to Kindle's relaunch, with Bezos on the set. "It's absolutely my new most favorite thing in the world," she crowed.[20] Sales took off.

The Aftermath of "Yes, We Can!"

At the original 2007 Kindle launch, Bezos had dropped a bombshell on the publishing industry. "*New York Times* bestsellers and new releases are only nine dollars and ninety-nine cents."[21] There was immediate confusion among the publishers, who'd not been told how Amazon was planning to price their e-books. Was it temporary? Permanent? Only for bestsellers?

The new low price for top e-books eventually and relentlessly began tilting the playing field toward digital. It put pressure on physical booksellers, threatened independent bookstores, and gave Amazon increased power in both the physical and digital book markets. That market power led over time to further concessions that were passed on to Amazon consumers in lower prices and cheaper shipping, hence more market share and even more leverage over the publishers. From Amazon's point of view, it was a virtuous circle; for the publishers, not so much.

Why was the Kindle successful? Russ Grandinetti, who has run content for Kindle for many years, puts it simply. "I think the reason Kindle succeeded while others failed is that we were obsessive, not about trying to build the sexiest gadget in the world, but rather about building something that actually fulfilled what people wanted."[22] Amazon had integrated its bookstore into the device, bringing the reading of e-books into the mainstream.

Whose insight was that? Bezos's! Says Grandinetti, quoting technology expert Alan Kay: "The best way to predict the future is to invent it."[23] If you don't have the competencies, hire them. What about the conventional rules? Who cares! "Yes, we can!" indeed!

Arnold Correia Said, "Yes, We Can!" Time After Time[24]

It was a sunny October morning in São Paulo in 2004, and SubWay Link founder and CEO Arnold Correia was facing a dilemma. He'd uncovered an opportunity to dramatically change the nature of his company's event production and management

"Change came easy to Correia, as he'd already reinvented the business once before, so change was not the issue."

business. Change came easy to Correia, as he'd already reinvented the business once before, so change was not the issue. But neither he nor his team knew anything about satellite transmission technology, which would be crucial if he proceeded.

The First "Yes, We Can!"

Ten years earlier, Correia had decided that producing lavish Sunday parties for Brazilian teenagers—*domingueiras*, as they were called—and managing a local rock band wasn't going to meet his career aspirations. He decided to redirect the event management skills he had developed toward the corporate market. He placed a small ad and a few days later he heard back from McDonald's, which was expanding rapidly throughout Brazil. McDonald's needed production services for an upcoming event. In a fast-food market that had grown rapidly in Brazil in recent years, the company needed to motivate and train its growing workforce.

Correia decided to take an unusual approach. "I put together a quote for a standard display and sound system, but if I won the contract, I planned to upgrade the size of the monitors and the quality of the speakers. I really wanted to impress them with an element of surprise to make a lasting impression in hopes of working with them in the future."[25]

The strategy worked. McDonald's was happy, as the event exceeded its expectations. Correia won lots of follow-on work for McDonald's thereafter, including board meetings, sales strategy conferences, motivational conferences, and more. Word spread. Soon Correia and his small team were producing events for some of the largest and fastest growing companies in Brazil.

In 1995, the first Walmart store opened in Brazil. Correia won a job for a promotional event, but the video production company Walmart had hired did not show up, so Correia was asked if he could do it. "Sure, we can!" replied Correia with his usual confidence, though Correia had neither shot nor edited a video in his life. "I frantically called all of my friends to help me find someone who could record video. Forty minutes later I found someone who could help, but in the strangest place. I had to pick him up at the cemetery, as it was the Day of the Dead, a Christian holiday in Brazil, which commemorated the faithful departed."[26] With video capabilities on board, Correia's company became a one-stop-shop provider for event production and for producing the corporate video as well.

The Second "Yes, We Can!"

Nearly a decade later and unbeknownst to Correia, in mid-2004 he was nominated for an entrepreneurship competition whose purpose was to choose the best young entrepreneurs in "the new Brazil." But Correia did not win. "It really bothered me. I wanted to know why we lost, so I asked one of the judges to tell me why we didn't win. It was the most valuable advice I have ever received." She was forthright. "The business you are in is not right for you; your ambition and drive is bigger than your industry. Your company, as it is now, is not scalable."[27]

Disappointed, but not deterred, Correia next traveled to the United States to see how retailers like his Brazilian clients were innovating elsewhere. He discovered that Walmart used a corporate TV network to motivate, inform and train employees at its

US stores. Even better, Correia learned that the network had not been built in-house. Walmart had contracted the service with an external supplier.

Corporate TV, as Walmart was using it, consisted of generating video content and broadcasting it, typically in real time, to multiple locations. Included were sales strategy updates, weekly motivational speeches to the sales staff, results announcements, training, and more.

Correia saw the opportunity as a game changer for his company. His idea was to start with one far-flung retail chain, perhaps Walmart or home appliance retailer Magazine Luiza. Each had more than 200 stores scattered around Brazil, and both were growing fast, as Brazil's economic boom continued to gather momentum. Instead of revenues depending on one-off events and video production, corporate TV could generate recurring monthly revenue. No longer would he have to wonder where the next project would come from. And it would leverage some of his company's existing capabilities and customer connections.

But he identified three obstacles. First, Brazil's Internet infrastructure was certainly not ready for streaming

❝But he identified three obstacles.❞

video. Satellite transmission would be the only way. Securing satellite bandwidth meant winning regulatory approval from the Brazilian government, which would involve extensive costs and an unknown period of time to obtain. Second, logistics. SubWay Link would have to install satellite and electronic equipment in remote locations all over Brazil. To date, his company had only done events in São Paulo. Third, funding. Roberto Bocchi, Correia's trusted number two since his *domingueiras* days, estimated the investment required at least 12 million *reais*, about US$4 million. SubWay Link had only 1 million *reais* cash on its balance sheet.

Correia was determined. He and his team prepared a business plan to show to his client Luiza Helena, CEO at the home appliance retail chain Magazine Luiza, whom he had already served in events and video production. "I have an idea how to grow my business," he told Luiza, "and I would welcome your advice."

Shrewdly, he titled the business plan "Corporate TV Proposal for Walmart Brazil." His goal wasn't to sell the project to Walmart, however, but to Magazine Luiza. "Why not Magazine Luiza?" Helena said upon seeing the proposal, grasping the idea's potential at once.

Overcoming the Obstacles

In early 2005, Correia put the majority of his US$1 million in savings back into the business; he also pledged his home and his business as collateral for equipment financing to the consternation of his wife, Bárbara. Not entirely happy with this turn of events, Bárbara, who had been an engineer with a leading Brazilian TV station, recommended a specialist, Herbe Zambrone, who could provide her husband with some sorely needed expertise.

Bárbara's broadcasting industry contacts resolved the technology challenges, too. Correia convinced a satellite owner she knew, who had spare capacity, to let SubWay Link use its license at the outset, thereby avoiding a lengthy delay. Soon thereafter, Zambrone learned that in Franca, a small inland city, there was no wait for licenses. Correia set up his broadcast hub there and SubWay Link soon won a license of its own.

The logistics were more difficult, but Correia promoted Thales Morales, a long-time staffer in video production, to lead the logistics effort. Thanks to Morales and his team, the Luiza operation was up and running, with 180 stores installed, by the agreed 60-day deadline. Later, Helena herself said of SubWay Link: "We have lots of things in common, like boldness and innovation. We are proud to have the first corporate TV system in Brazil. I appreciate SubWay Link's ability to go further and to win the challenge to constantly outperform expectations."[28] Not long thereafter, Walmart-Brazil came on board, too.

The Third "Yes, We Can!"

In late 2009, after narrowly scrap-
ing through the global financial crisis, Correia was only partially happy
with his new Corporate TV business. "The clients were very satisfied
with the services we provided. But I
was worried that we were still on the
cost side of their businesses." The

**ff The financial crisis
had taught Correia
that, "In difficult
times, costs always get
cut." He wondered if
he couldn't change his
model again.**

financial crisis had taught Correia that, "In difficult times, costs
always get cut." He wondered if he could change his model again.
"I want to be part of the revenue for my customers."[29]

Observing what was happening elsewhere, Correia again
saw something he could adapt to Brazil: Digital Out-Of-Home
Television. DOOH-TV consisted of providing infrastructure
and content to be broadcast inside a client's premises, but targeting their customers, rather than their employees, as his current
Corporate TV offering did.

In the United States, Walmart's provider sold DOOH-TV
time to advertisers, including Walmart's own suppliers, plus
credit-card issuers, mobile-phone operators, and others. Walmart
was granted some of the time for its own advertising and received
a commission on all media sales. Clearly, the service offered some
synergy with corporate TV and would take advantage of some of
the company's current assets and capabilities, unlike some of
Correia's earlier moves. But three challenges were immediately apparent:

- **Market:** Would Brazilian retailers welcome such a service?
  Would advertisers buy?
- **Production:** SubWay Link had always produced special-
  ized content, and never for broadcast to ordinary consum-
  ers. Lots of content would be required to fill each day.
  Licensing third-party content would probably be required.

- **Financing:** SubWay Link's balance sheet remained precarious, with little cash on hand, though the company had returned to positive cash flow.

Realizing that his likely customers for DOOH-TV were already his clients in Corporate TV and that DOOH-TV would pay their bills and perhaps increase their sales, Correia proceeded full speed ahead. Walmart signed on. By 2012, Walmart-Brazil's revenue share from DOOH-TV contributed some 11 percent of its full-year profit!

In 2013, Correia changed the name of his company to Atmo Digital to better represent what the business had become. By 2017, Atmo Digital had become one of Brazil's largest out-of-home media companies with more than 18,000 screens in more than 1,000 locations. "Yes, we can!" had transformed Correia's company, not once, but three times!

MOVE Guides Strays and Stumbles[30]

I'd like to be able to tell you that straying from one's knitting and finding or acquiring new competencies is easy to do and guaranteed to succeed. Of course, I cannot. And it is not. Most new products fail.[31]

MOVE Guides founder Brynne Kennedy had personally experienced the relocation difficulties that arose for those pursuing careers in international companies. Her journey had taken her from her native United States to Hong Kong, Delhi, back to Hong Kong, then Singapore. In 2010 she stepped off the career treadmill to pursue an MBA in London, with the idea of starting a business that would address the hassles with which she'd become so intimately familiar. In 2012 the business got started.

Choosing a Path

By early 2014, Kennedy had raised nearly $2 million of seed capital, written a series of short guides (MOVE Guides) for several cities around the world, and built a website. The idea was to use software to take the hassle—hassle for those who moved, and hassle for the corporate HR professionals who supported them—out of international moves. Which are the best (or cheapest) moving companies? How do I open a bank account? What about taxes? And much more.

For the person moving, there were three elements to the proposition:

1. Web-based content to aid in discovering what one needed to know about a new location
2. Vetting and connecting movers with trusted suppliers and contracting for their service
3. A web-based checklist for the move

Most multinational companies had HR professionals tasked with supporting such moves. Senior executives received expensive, tailored, white-glove managed moves from HR and from the relocation management companies (RMCs) to whom everything was outsourced. But the more numerous moves of junior employees were handled differently. HR would give the employee a lump-sum payment, and the employees would have to manage things on their own. Not only were the relocating employees not entirely happy with the hassle that they were required to self-manage, but the HR people felt guilty about the lack of care that lump-sum moves entailed. And lump-sum moves meant that the employees were not able to hit the ground running in their new jobs while they handled the myriad of tasks that international moves always required.

After conducting considerable research, Kennedy and her team decided to focus on the lump-sum moves segment, as that was where the greatest pain-point seemed to lie. "It had become clear that lump-sum moves were a problem for everyone," explained Kennedy.[32] Some RMCs serviced this market segment as a favor to their managed-moves clients, but they did not like doing so, as typical fees were only $500 per move.

By August 2014, Kennedy had won several pilots with high-profile clients and had converted two such clients into paying customers. The employees were consistently delighted with the support they received from MOVE Guides. And the HR professionals were happy that their employees were happy. Kennedy and her team began to realize how unhappy many companies were with the services of the RMCs. "They really liked our technology platform but wanted a full-service product that serviced *all* types of moves, not just lump-sum moves," recalled Kennedy's co-founder, Steve Black.[33]

> **The unit economics were not panning out in the lump-sum segment. A pivot seemed called for.**

Their customers' requests for moving up to the managed-moves segment fell on welcome ears, as the unit economics were not panning out in the lump-sum segment. A pivot seemed called for. "We initially forecasted £800 in average revenue per move from supplier commissions," Black reported to Kennedy, "and we figured we'd turn profitable in our 12th month in business." But the average revenue per move was running less than one-third of projections. Relocated employees were couch-surfing with friends, often moving only what the airlines would let them take along as baggage, and pocketing as much of the lump sum payment as they could! MOVE Guides was burning cash and burning it fast.

"Yes, We Can!"

Kennedy and Black conferred with their team. "Like everything else we've done so far, we could figure this out," said Kennedy. Black chimed in with what it would take to make the move:

We would need more cash to staff up the services side of the business, similar to a concierge-type support for those relocating. We'd also need a much more sophisticated back-office and CRM system for our MOVE Advocates to offer a more white-glove service. But think of the value-add we could offer as a software *and* services company. I've run some numbers, and taking on managed moves will enable us to grow our bookings and top-line revenue much faster, though the manpower to provide white-glove service to the managed moves segment means that our losses would also likely grow.[34]

VP of Engineering Steve Giles was reticent. "But guys, we haven't even figured out how to make the lump-sum product run well. And, we don't even know what this managed move product is supposed to do!" Giles agreed that, while managed moves looked attractive, such a change would be challenging. "Taking on managed moves is a different beast," he argued. "From a technology standpoint lump-sum moves are easy. It's software and we just manage the platform. But managed moves is platform plus services."[35] Did MOVE Guides have the necessary competencies to operate a white glove services business? We'll soon see.

Kennedy next reached out to her lead venture capital investor, who saw taking on the managed moves business as an opportunity. It would provide crucial short-term revenue, he argued, and it would be easier to cross-sell lump-sum move solutions once managed moves were being done. "We were getting ready to raise a Series A round," recalled Kennedy. "In the venture capital world if you don't get Series A funding from the VC firms that gave you seed capital, it's like a big scarlet letter. So, I knew we needed to work hard to keep them happy."[36] With her investors and most of her team on board with the decision to take on managed moves, and with managed moves comprising a much larger market than lump-sum in value terms, Kennedy and Black said, "Go!"

Things Unravel

Steve Giles and his team of engineers went into high gear to keep up with a dramatically increased workload. "Resourcing was only half the problem. The other half was actually figuring out what we were trying to build," recalled Giles. "We needed a minimum viable product, which we could then innovate on top of. But instead we slid into a reactive mode, with the sales team promising a lot to clients and then my team having to sprint to deliver solutions that individual customers wanted."[37]

> **By mid-2015, despite adding 30 new clients, the company was rapidly burning through cash.**

MOVE Guides also needed to ramp up the number of MOVE Advocates to service managed moves. This added cost, and complexity, too. By mid-2015, despite adding 30 new clients, the company was rapidly burning through cash, "And gross profit had slipped below 50% from 70+% at the beginning of the year," fumed Kennedy.[38]

By mid-2016, things clearly weren't working. "Sales started taking longer than expected to close, but I couldn't pin down if it was because we didn't have the right salespeople, or if it was the product."[39] Kennedy set out to raise capital once more. Everywhere she went, she heard concerns about the business model and scalability. "Everyone loved the category, strategy, vision and product. But their challenges really came down to the fact that they believed our business model and MOVE Advocate service model weren't scalable. The VCs would come in and sit down with a MOVE Advocate, and then tell us they had concerns." She went to her board and told them they needed to take this feedback seriously. "I've had 25 meetings with the top 25 VC funds in the world, and they're all saying the same thing."[40]

Game Over

In 2017, with MOVE Guides burning more than $1 million per month in cash, the board pulled the plug. Straying from the company's original lump-sum-moves knitting was simply not working out. Expenses were cut to the bone. New management came in. Yet another strategy was put in place, which involved selling the managed moves business and refocusing on software. Another software firm working in the relocation software arena and a technology shop were acquired. Early investors were washed out, and the company was rebranded as Topia. Will Topia survive where MOVE Guides could not? Time will tell.

Lessons Learned for Times When You Yearn to Say, "Yes, We Can!"

Saying "Yes, we can!" transformed Amazon from a still emerging e-commerce retailer into a technology-driven behemoth that would go on to bring the world Amazon Web Services, Alexa, and more. Saying "Yes, we can!" transformed SubWay Link three times into a leading role in Brazil's out-of-home media industry. But saying "Yes, we can!" to an ill-advised expansion into a business in which it lacked both competencies and a viable business model cost MOVE Guides its survival as a stand-alone entity. Whether you're an entrepreneur or an employee in somebody else's business that's trying to be counter-conventional, what are the lessons that these case studies provide?

On the importance of customer insight and understanding in "Yes, we can!" moves: Amazon's hiring of Pentagram to help it "understand the physics of reading" together with Jeff Bezos's insistence that the device provide instant access to practically any book—anywhere, anytime—were central to its ability to develop an e-reader that consumers would flock to in droves. More fundamentally, Amazon's culture of obsessing over the customer and working backwards from what the customer wants and needs has given us innovation after innovation—think Amazon Prime—that has set Amazon apart from virtually all its competitors.

Arnold Correia's mantra of "under promise and over deliver" helped his young company get a foot in the door with large corporate clients and keep it there. Giving great customer service is something that's easy to say, but exceedingly difficult for many companies to do. Do it well, and your customers will stick around.

❝Could Kennedy and Black have discovered up front that lump-sum movers don't typically spend much of the lump sum?❞ Contrast these customer-first strengths with MOVE Guides' lack of understanding of its first target user, the lump-sum mover. Could Kennedy and Black have discovered up front that lump-sum movers don't typically spend much of the lump sum, preferring to pocket as much of the cash as they can? Probably! Did they? No.

On the importance of viable business models: Note also how the MOVE Guides' founders appeared to have been blinded by what on its surface appeared to be a large managed moves market. Entrepreneurs love large markets, of course. So do corporates. But there is much more to a viable business than a large market, which some prospective customers are asking you to serve.[41]

Thus, among the most crucial elements to understand in a "Yes, we can!" move is whether the unit economics and the business model itself actually stack up.[42] For MOVE Guides, unfortunately, the unit economics in the lump-sum moves segment didn't pan out, because those who moved preferred to keep most of the lump-sum payment rather than spend it; and trying to replace tailored white-glove managed moves service with subscription software sold via a SaaS model was arguably never going to work.

Jeff Bezos, on the other hand, saw that digitally bringing an entire library of books to the Kindle at a moment's notice would vastly increase its revenue and profit potential. Not only was that what the customer wanted, he foresaw, but it would dramatically improve the business model for Kindle.

On accessing new competencies: At heart of the "Yes, we can!" statement is a follow-on question, often unstated. "Holy cow! How on earth will we do that?" It's an implicit acknowledgment that one is about to stray from one's past knitting, with new competencies, capabilities, networks, or something else required. As we've seen in this chapter, there are three ways to acquire them. Hire them. Acquire them, via an M&A transaction, as Amazon did with the Mobipocket acquisition. Or beg or borrow them, as you'll read more about in Chapter 6. Let's explore each of these approaches.

Hiring people with new competencies you will soon require is always a challenge. In part, that's because one who lacks those competencies is probably not a good judge of others who might—or might not—possess them! How does one with an idea for a new digital venture, but who lacks digital competencies, for example, assess candidates who might bring the digital competencies required. Not easily!

Amazon's solution to the hiring challenge, an interviewing and selection process dubbed "Bar-Raiser," had already been developed.[43] Its purpose was to minimize the variability inherent in most ad-hoc hiring processes and avoid the urgency bias that could result in substandard hires or leadership hires who were unlikely to operate within Amazon's leadership principles. As I write more than 17 years later, Amazon's Gregg Zehr remains president of Lab126. Not only can new core competencies be acquired and developed, in spite of the conventional rules to the contrary, they might even stick around for the long term!

Another solution to the hiring challenge is to reach out to one's network and find trusted referrals. That's how SubWay

Link's Arnold Correia found Herbe Zambrone to bring in-house the competencies it required to get into Corporate TV.

Accessing new competencies via the merger and acquisition route provides another source of new competencies. When Amazon acquired the 10-person French company Mobipocket for the e-reading software competencies it lacked, it brought on the entire team and handed over to them full responsibility to further develop the necessary software, for which Mobipocket already had a strong start. Gutsy? Perhaps. But it worked. This practice is now sufficiently common that it has a name of its own, "acquihire."[44]

The third way to access new competencies is to "beg, borrow, or steal" them, as we saw when SubWay Link leased spare satellite capacity on an existing satellite, rather than having to get a government license for its own capacity. You'll learn much more about borrowing the competencies or other assets you might need in Chapter 6. This approach is typically highly capital-efficient, and a good way to get started in an uncertain venture. Many entrepreneurs' mindsets think and act this way; many corporate routines don't, given their assumption that to get into something new, they must "invest." But why invest, if you can beg or borrow?

On organizing the business to take full advantage of the "Yes, we can!" opportunity at hand: Jeff Bezos, arguably, is among the most opportunity-focused entrepreneurs the world has seen. Books sold on the Internet, then e-readers and e-books, then "everything," now space travel and more. But Bezos is very much down to earth in how he organizes the pursuit of such opportunities large or small. Virtually anything new at Amazon is pursued by what's known as a "two pizza team." That's a team small enough to be fed for lunch by two pizzas.[45] Small autonomous teams, given full-time responsibility to develop the opportunity, with agreed metrics so that progress can be measured.

Bezos's second key organizing principle, as we saw in the Kindle project, is that the responsibility for something new is not embedded within the existing organizational structure. It's managed by an entirely separate organization. In Bezos's view, that was the only way to get single-minded attention focused on something that was dramatically new. We'll see this principle put to work by Nestlé in Chapter 4.

❝❝As the saying goes, if you've got a hammer, every problem looks like a nail. ❞❞

On choosing investors for "Yes, we can!" projects: As we saw with MOVE Guides, alongside additional competencies sometimes additional capital is required to pursue a new opportunity. I've learned over the years that different investors like to invest in different kinds of deals. As the saying goes, if you've got a hammer, every problem looks like a nail. Once you've brought a certain kind of investor into your company, it's likely to see things that look like its kind of "nails."

Had MOVE Guides not chosen investors who liked to invest in enterprise software and SaaS companies, the company's strategy might have developed differently in its early years. Perhaps its early struggles in getting enough revenue out of lump-sum moves might have encouraged it to pivot and move into a marketplace business, an Airbnb for international moves, in some sense. That's something that Kennedy and Black had considered earlier but rejected. Once enterprise and SaaS investors were on board, that kind of strategy was probably off the table.

The MOVE Guides experience is one reason that I encourage entrepreneurs to bring on talent for the competencies required as early as possible, but to take on investment as late as possible. Once investors are on board, you may be locked into a path that may turn out to be the wrong one. Better to bootstrap the business in its early days and get funding from customers' revenue, until traction is proven. Once a proven path has been discovered, that's a better time to add fuel.[46]

On recovering when "Yes, we can!" fails to work out: We've seen that a "Yes, we can!" mindset does not always lead to success. So, what should you do if your new business or project is not panning out? You'll need to make sure you understand why it's not working, for which you'll need sound metrics in place to help. But in four words, sometimes you must "fail fast and move on!" That's not what MOVE Guides did. It burned investors' cash for years in what, we now know, was a fruitless journey to make the managed-moves business work.

How to Add "Yes, We Can!" to *Your* Entrepreneurial Mindset

As the case studies in this chapter demonstrate, saying "Yes, we can!" to something that's entirely new often comes down to getting the right new people "on the bus," as author Jim Collins calls it.[47] In Collins's view, first you get the right people on the bus. Then you let them figure out where to drive it. That's exactly what Jeff Bezos did to create the Kindle. People first, product and strategy later. So what should you do now in order to prepare yourself for a "Yes, we can!" moment?

First you'll need to muster up your self-confidence, some bravery, even audacity, perhaps. Some call it seeing the cup as half-full, rather than half-empty. If you're an entrepreneur already on your journey, you probably have some of these attributes already. If you're an innovator within an established business, you probably have them, too. But that's not sufficient for putting yourself in position to say "Yes, we can!" when the opportunity arises.

As the case studies in this chapter demonstrate, the best way to identify the people you'll want on your bus is through your network. That includes your professional network; your school or alumni network; your social media network on LinkedIn and others; your friends and family; even your spouse, as we saw with Arnold Correia. The subject of how to build your network is more than we can take on here in a few paragraphs, so I suggest you read one or more books like these:[48]

- *Superconnector*, by Scott Gerber and Ryan Paugh
- *Never Eat Alone*, by Keith Ferrazi and Tahl Raz
- *Giftology*, by John Ruhlin
- *The 7 Habits of Highly Effective People*, by Stephen Covey
- *Networking Is Not Working*, by Derek Coburn
- *Give and Take*, by Adam Grant
- *How to Win Friends and Influence People*, by Dale Carnegie

Any of these titles should get you on your way to building and maintaining a network that can help you source the talent, the skills, the capabilities you'll need when your "Yes, we can!" moment arrives and you muster up the courage to be counter-conventional and break the rules. Maybe you won't even need a trip to the nearest cemetery to meet them!

Your growing network will not only help you identify and assess talent you may require. It will also keep you abreast of what's going on in the market you serve and the industry in which you play. That's how the Amazon team knew of Mobipocket in far-away France. Build your network and thrive!

Closing Thoughts

I don't intend to say in this chapter that sticking to your knitting or building upon and enhancing your competencies is something to be avoided, of course. If your competencies will take you where you want to go, as they have for companies like Honda and 3M, that's great news. But as you've seen in this chapter, a "Yes, we can!" mindset is a potentially powerful way to transform your company, whether a big one where you work or a business of your own, and set it onto a growth path to the moon, if all goes well, despite the conventional advice that you should stick to your knitting. Thus, a few questions for you: Can you learn to say "Yes, we can!" at opportune moments? Can you take steps to make sure that the right people, the customer insights, the right unit economics, and a viable business model can be put into place to give you a fighting chance for success? Can you break the "stick to your knitting" rule and succeed? Yes, you can!

3

It's the Customer's Problem That Matters, Not Your Solution: Problem-First, Not Product-First, Logic

Long-time venture capital investor and Silicon Valley observer Bill Joy put it simply back in 2004: "Let's be blunt. Big companies almost never innovate. It's not that innovation is rare—it's occurring everywhere. Which means, mostly, elsewhere."[1]

My family has been a user of Tide laundry detergent for decades. We've seen Tide add blue speckles, to get our clothes "cleaner." Remove them, to make our clothes "fresher." Add green ones, then scents, add water so it pours; and so on. Is this what passes for innovation? Really?

Procter & Gamble, Tide's maker, seems to be forever tinkering with its product formulations. Take P&G's Crest toothpaste, for example. It is now offered in so many varieties that it makes my head spin when I—or my wife, Donna, who prefers a different variety—need to buy another tube at the grocery store.

This product-first logic is the conventional way of life in business today: product line extensions (Coke, Diet Coke, Coke Zero, Vanilla and Cherry Coke, Coke Natural: what will Coke think of next?); product improvements or modifications like those of Tide (always "new and improved"); brand extensions (Hewlett-Packard branded paper for your printer); and more.

New products matter, but . . .: To be fair, new products, it is said, are the lifeblood of long-term business success. They constitute a key mechanism by which companies attempt to adapt to the ever-changing wants and needs of customers and consumers, and the increasingly volatile market and industry settings in which they compete.[2] It's no wonder, then, that so many companies go to great lengths to develop and introduce one new product after another.

Sadly, however, most new products fail. They fail to deliver sufficient value or function to the intended customer, so too few customers buy them. They fail to deliver the return on investment that was hoped for by their makers. Sometimes, they simply fail to work as intended. At the root of these failures, I argue, is the fact that most new products don't resolve a compelling enough problem—in the customer's eyes, not the seller's—that they deserve to live on.

Entrepreneurs think differently: Vinod Khosla, a long-time VC investor, begs to differ from this conventional big-company, product-first wisdom. "Any big problem is a big opportunity," Khosla says. "If you think about it, no problem, no solution, no company. It's very simple. Every big problem is a big opportunity. If you don't have a big problem, you don't have a big opportunity. Nobody will pay you to solve a non-problem."[3] Khosla's problem-first—rather than product-first—logic is the driving force behind many entrepreneurs and their sometimes surprisingly promising new ventures that break the conventional product-first rules. "Why didn't I think of that?" some observers wonder in hindsight.

> **"If you don't have a big problem, you don't have a big opportunity. Nobody will pay you to solve a non-problem."**

What's on tap in Chapter 3: In this chapter, we'll examine the now-forgotten story about how today's global leader in athletic shoes and other sports gear, Nike, got its start by solving two key problems that its initial target market, elite distance runners, felt viscerally. We'll follow with the story of Simon Cohen, a young Mexican entrepreneur who was fed up with the poor service that freight forwarders were providing to his family's textile business. We'll then observe how an American entrepreneur, Jon Thorne, built a thriving business based on technology that enabled plastic surgeons to work faster and with more precise outcomes, and neurosurgeons to conduct brain surgery without their surgical instruments sticking to brain cells. After all, you'd not be very happy with your surgeon if your new appearance was scarred, or the doctor removed more brain cells than necessary!

To examine the unfortunate consequences of product-first logic, we'll also explore what happens when product–market fit for a new kind of ski boot simply fails to materialize: the product struggles to gain traction and the business goes nowhere, often excruciatingly, painfully slowly. In my experience, product-first companies are prone to becoming the "living dead," as some investors call them, consuming never-ending amounts of management effort, and sometimes round after round of investment capital, too, all to little effect. The cautionary tale of Apex Ski Boots will certainly not inspire you, but it may well exhaust you.

As always, to wrap up the chapter, we'll then pull together the lessons that this chapter's case studies deliver. Finally, whether you're a swashbuckling entrepreneur or a leader hoping to make the company where you work more counter-conventional in its approach, I'll suggest some steps you can take now to add problem-first logic to *your* entrepreneurial mindset. Let's go!

Distance Runners' Problems: Philip Knight to the Rescue[4]

When you're able to run nearly a four-minute mile, as Philip Knight was in his youth, you know what it takes to reach that level of performance—mile after mile of training, day after day. But it's not mile after mile running laps on a smooth track. It's mile after mile on country roads and narrow trails in the woods, up hills and down. The continuing pounding takes its toll on distance runners' legs, especially their shins and Achilles tendons. The uneven terrain—littered with rocks, sticks, rodent holes, and more—leads to sprained ankles far too often. Problems, indeed, leading to a special set of needs, as Knight knew personally.

Knight, fresh out of business school in 1962, had written a research paper on the shoe industry for an entrepreneurship class. He had already been aware that Japanese brands had made deep inroads into the camera industry, once dominated by German companies. He argued in his research paper that "Japanese running shoes might do the same thing."[5]

The current German shoes weren't fit for purpose, in his view, as far as distance runners' needs were concerned. Knight wanted to offer shoes that were explicitly designed with *distance* runners' needs in mind. He wanted shoes with more cushioning, to ease the stress—and the all-too-frequent shin splints, stress fractures, and the like—of all those miles, with a wider footbed, to provide more lateral stability, thereby preventing at least some of the inevitable ankle sprains.

> **❝Knight wanted to offer shoes that were explicitly designed with *distance* runners' needs in mind.❞**

Reaching out to his former running coach at the University of Oregon, Bill Bowerman, Knight showed Bowerman some shoe samples that he'd procured from Onitsuka Company in Kobe, Japan. Onitsuka's Tigers held potential, Knight believed. Bowerman agreed. "Those Japanese shoes," he said. "They're pretty good. How about letting me in on the deal?"[6]

Bowerman, an inveterate tinkerer, was always messing around with his athletes' shoes. What he was after, among other things, was lighter weight shoes, in order to speed up his runners' race times. An ounce here and an ounce there, multiplied by the number of steps a distance runner runs in a mile or a marathon, adds up to a surprising amount of additional exertion that his runners—equipped with the right shoes, of course—would not have to undertake. Onitsuka's Tigers would have to be tweaked, and tweaked again.

Blue Ribbon Sports Embarks

Knight's and Bowerman's fledgling company, Blue Ribbon Sports, managed to sell 1,300 pairs of Tigers in its first year for a meager $8,000 in revenue. Paying the founders a salary wasn't going to happen any time soon. Knight, having by then passed all four parts of the CPA exam, decided he'd better get a day job as an accountant. "I was officially and irrevocably a card-carrying bean counter," he recalled.[7]

In the autumn of 1965, after every race, Bowerman could be found madly scribbling notes on not one, but two kinds of performance: that of his runners and that of their new Tiger shoes. Meanwhile, the duo had managed to scrape together the resources to open two retail stores, one in Santa Monica, California, whose stockroom did double duty as the company's warehouse; the other in Eugene, Oregon, near Bowerman's University of Oregon campus. By the close of 1966, annual sales had grown tenfold to a still modest $84,000.

The Waffle Sole Attacks the Customer Problems

In 1971, though Blue Ribbon would finish the year with $1.3 million in sales, Knight was worried. It was becoming clear that, for a variety of reasons, Blue Ribbon Sports and its manufacturing partner, Onitsuka, were headed for a breakup. That meant new shoe designs, and a new brand, too. Nike, the Greek goddess of victory, was born as a shoe brand.

But it wasn't just Knight doing the worrying, despite the innovations in midsole cushioning and lightweight uppers that his company had pioneered. Meeting with Bowerman after yet another trip to Japan, Knight and his number two, Bob Woodell, pointed out, "The outer sole of the training shoe hadn't changed in fifty years."[8] The treads were still waves or grooves across the bottom of the foot. Bowerman had been wrestling with the fact that his runners were not getting full benefit from the new, spongy, polyurethane tracks that were coming into favour, one of which had just been installed at Bowerman's university. His runners' shoes simply weren't gripping the new surface right. It was yet another problem to solve. But how?

The next Sunday, at breakfast with his wife, Bowerman connected the dots of Woodell's and Knight's observation with the grid-like pattern of his wife's waffle iron. Pouring some leftover urethane into the waffle iron after breakfast, Bowerman promptly ruined it. Undeterred, a few iterations later, he held in his hands some squares of hard rubber with nubs. Sewing a pair of soles hand-cut from one of the squares to a pair of running shoes, he gave them to one of his runners. "The runner laced them on and ran like a rabbit," Bowerman reported.[9] As Knight would recall years later, Bowerman had made history, "Remaking an industry, transforming the way athletes would run and stop and jump for generations. I wonder if he could conceive in that moment all that he'd done. All that would follow. I know I couldn't."[10]

By 1976, the waffle trainer was becoming a cultural artefact. And it was winning races, too. At the trials for the 1976 US Olympics team, Nike-shod runners took first, second, and third in the 10,000 meters; first in the 5,000 meters; and first in the marathon. No medals in that year's Olympics in Atlanta, however. That year, sales doubled again, to $14 million.

Run, Stop, Jump

By now the rest of the Nike story is familiar history to any sports fan or weekend athlete. Depending on the sport, an athlete's feet are required to do different things. Some feet just run, whether sprinting around a 400-meter track or on a 100-yard straightaway, or running a 26.2 mile marathon. Some feet—tennis players', for example—stop suddenly and change direction on a dime. Others—as in basketball—jump and land on the hard surface of a basketball court.

For each of these sports, the nature of what's entailed in competing at a high level poses problems, problems that better footwear can potentially solve—for elite athletes and weekend warriors alike. Reducing injuries for distance runners while aiding faster race times. Providing better traction for instant changes in direction for tennis players. And so on. Identifying such problems has enabled the Nike team to develop innovations that have led its industry for many years. Problem-first. The product innovation then follows.

The Foundation of Nike's Success

The capabilities that Nike—née Blue Ribbon Sports—developed over its first decade in business served it well: how to design shoes that meet different athletes' needs; how to get them manufactured in Asia; how to engage college coaches, and then professional athletes, to gain credibility; how to build a brand. But at the heart of it all, Phil Knight's focus on solving problems for athletes provided the foundation upon which his company was built.

On December 2, 1980, nearly 18 years to the day after Knight's first exploratory trip to Japan, Nike went public, selling its shares in an Initial Public Offering at the same $22 price per share as another upstart company, Apple Computer, 10 days later. Days later, Nike's stock had overtaken Apple and surged into the lead. Problem-first logic that met the needs of elite athletes—as well as everyday athletes—in one sport after another, coupled with shrewd and inventive marketing, had served Nike very well.

Simon Cohen: Freight Forwarding Service Need Not Be So Bad[11]

Simon Cohen, fresh out of university in 1996, joined his father's textile company in Monterrey, Mexico as Import/Export Manager. His role was to build up the international side of the family business, which seemed a good idea in the wake of the NAFTA free-trade agreement that Mexico, the United States, and Canada had agreed on in 1994.

Importing and exporting textiles meant that Cohen relied on a freight forwarder, one recommended by a friend, to organize the necessary carriers and manage the shipments. Big problem!

The service from the freight forwarding company was very poor. My first order was sending 14 cubic meters of goods to Costa Rica. We didn't know anything about timing because they didn't keep us updated, the goods got damaged, and we hadn't been advised about insurance, so we lost money. This company had been recommended to us, but it was terrible. I tried 10 others, but they were all bad.[12]

Having been introduced to two German immigrants, Manfred Jaekel and Thomas Kroeger, who were running a small freight forwarding business in Mexico City, Cohen decided there was an opportunity to do likewise in Monterrey. He set out to provide better service than the current players were offering. After asking his father for three months off to give the new venture a try, he struck a deal with the Germans. Cohen would seek business in Monterrey, and the Germans' company, Cargo Masters International (CMI), would handle the shipments. Profits would be split. By late 1997, the partnership was handling 20–30 containers per month.

Jaekel was thrilled with Cohen's progress. "We're very surprised at what you've been able to do in Monterrey. We've been trying to get things to work there for a long time, but you've been able to do it in months."[13]

Cohen, too, was pleased. "Manfred acted as my mentor. He was a great teacher, explaining everything I needed to know, step by step. I took him to meet big clients, some of the biggest companies in Monterrey, and I wrote down everything he said to them during the sales process—and then 'copy-pasted' all of this when talking to my own customers."[14]

CMN Is Born

The Germans and the Cohens decided to formalize their relationship, and a new entity, Cargo Masters del Norte (CMN), was formed, 50 percent owned by the Germans and 50 percent by the Cohens. In 1999, in its first full year of trading, revenue was $1.1 million. CMN was on its way!

By then, Cohen had learned that, much like his own early experience, many who needed freight moved from one place to another had recurring problems. Some shipments were late, delayed by bad weather, missed connections between one carrier and another, or other causes. Sometimes there was damage en route. If not properly insured, such damage could pose financial problems for the party expecting to receive the shipment in good condition.

Cohen discovered that addressing such client problems was actually an information issue. When something happened that was out of CMN's control, clients would typically understand, as long as they were kept informed and given options about how to rectify the situation where possible.

> In the early days, I took advantage of the time differences across the world. Each night, I set my alarm for 2 a.m., and spent an hour or so replying to emails, to give instructions to the shipping lines, talk to my agents, get cargo updates, and let customers know where their goods were. Then I would go back to sleep until the morning. For shipments from China, this meant I gained a day. While our competitors waited until the next day, we replied the same day. Some of our clients still phone me in the middle of the night for updates on their shipments. We are not a transport company, we are a service company. I can't control the vessels, trucks, trains and airplanes. The only thing I can do is to tell the truth and offer my customers as many choices as possible.[15]

As Cohen learned more about the freight forwarding business, he found other problems he could solve for his clients, too. For instance, most shipping lines would charge demurrage fees for their containers, starting from seven days after arrival at the port. But unloading and returning the container often took longer than anticipated. CMN began negotiating with carriers for a longer period in which containers could be unloaded. Pushing the deadline back to 15 or 28 days after arrival sometimes saved CMN clients thousands of dollars in fees.

CMN also offered a service whereby clients could leave empty containers in the destination city, rather than paying for their return to port. CMN would then fill the container with exporters' goods for the return journey, typically saving the client as much as 40 percent of inland freight costs.

Solving Customer Problems Through Superior Service

Cohen was discovering that offering superior service paid off in the long run. But, he recalls,

> Keeping customers happy wasn't always easy. When things went wrong, some customers would get very stressed. One customer in particular, the biggest snack manufacturer in Mexico, threatened to sue and to "break" my company after a plane accident in Brazil. The accident meant that promotional stickers would be missing from a production run of croissants. The company would have lost millions. I kept calm, and patiently explained what had happened. We offered the customer as many options as we could. We managed to do the impossible, and the stickers arrived only a few hours late—in time for the croissants. We lost a lot of money on that operation. A few years later, this company was bought by Pepsico, which was great for us, as now we are a great partner for them across all their business divisions.[16]

Growing CMN

By 2000, CMN was doubling its revenue year-on-year. Its core business had been driven initially by Mexican trade with Europe.

While Mexican exports to Europe lagged far behind those to the United States, European countries were the second largest importers of Mexican goods and services. But the world was changing. Cohen foresaw a greater role for China in world trade, including trade with Mexico. From that time forward, CMN managed increasing numbers of shipments across the Pacific Ocean, particularly from China, but also elsewhere in Southeast Asia.

By 2002, CMN had overtaken CMI in sales. It was becoming clear that different standards of service were offered to customers by the two branches. The Monterrey team lived closer to the office but commuting times in Mexico City typically exceeded two hours. Thus, office hours in the capital were much more limited. There were also differences in the respective office cultures. Thomas Kroeger had a somewhat brash management style, and sometimes made comments to his Mexico City employees that some thought inappropriate.

These differences in service levels meant that customers soon started to choose CMN over CMI. Cohen recalled, "We usually had people in the office from 8 a.m. until 9 p.m., and customers would often say, 'No one is answering the phone in Mexico City, so can you sort out our shipment.' Manfred and Thomas were happy for us to do the work, because they still earned the profits, but their staff was not."[17]

In 2007, the Germans and the Cohens decided to part ways. The Cohens acquired the Germans' share in CMN along with the right to begin doing business in Mexico City after 2009. The Germans continued to operate their business in Mexico City. In 2009, to avoid confusion in the marketplace, the Cohens rebranded CMN as Henco Logistics. By 2014, Henco's revenue from its new Mexico City office had surpassed that of Monterrey.

Problem-First Logic in a Service Business

By 2021, Henco had opened offices up and down the Pacific coast of Latin America and had become one of Latin America's most honored companies for its employee-focused work culture. Having never differentiated its offering based on price, and having never employed a sales force, Henco has grown rapidly and consistently by identifying problems that its clients have, and then providing superior service that addresses those problems.

Uniquely in its industry, Henco entrusts and empowers those handling shipments to handle client relations as well, including the acquisition of new clients, much of which arises from word-of-mouth referrals from other happy clients. Doing so ensures timely client communication when problems arise—as they inevitably do in the freight forwarding industry—and avoids internal bureaucracy in getting solutions identified and implemented.

Offering superb customer service is easy to say, and many companies say it; but it is devilishly difficult to deliver on a consistent basis. Henco, with thanks to its problem-first logic and employee-first culture, appears to have found a way.

> **Offering superb customer service is easy to say, and many companies say it; but it is devilishly difficult to deliver on a consistent basis.**

Jon Thorne: What If Surgical Instruments Did Not Stick?[18]

At age 37, Jon Thorne decided that putting his engineering and product design skills to work in his own company was a better way forward than doing the contract research and development (R&D) that he'd been doing for others. "I'd rather have the fate of my inventions in my own hands," he recalled.[19] A year earlier, Thorne had helped develop an electrosurgical probe whose purpose was to seal a new and innovative lung patch to human lungs ("Like patching a tire," as Thorne put it). With its proprietary silver alloy coating, the probe seared the patch to the lung without causing any sticking or tearing of tissue.

Unfortunately, however, Thorne's client ultimately abandoned the lung patch project, despite having won US Food and Drug Administration (FDA) approval for it. Believing in the potential of the product he'd engineered, Thorne struck a deal with his former client to license the probe and the silver alloy technology that underpinned its nonstick properties. Silverglide Surgical Technologies was born!

Customer Problems and Customer Feedback Show the Way

Electrosurgery involved the application of radio frequency energy to human tissue in order to stop bleeding, seal vessels, or dissect tissue. Electrosurgical instruments, in a wide variety of shapes and sizes, incorporated an electrode mechanism that would be placed in contact with the human tissue and convey the radio frequency energy to the patient.

Thorne already knew that the global electrosurgical instruments market had reached $578 million in 1997, which offered plenty of opportunity, in his view. Silverglide's licensed technology provided nonstick capabilities that did not deteriorate with reuse. It was, in Thorne's view, far superior to the disposable nonstick Teflon-coated instruments that had entered the market over the past decade, with only modest success.

With a product now in hand, Thorne's first move was to get some probes into the hands of a few surgeons to see what they thought of them. "Too large," said one surgeon. "It blocks my view of the surgical site." "I like how it doesn't stick," said another, "but it's a lot of trouble to have to disassemble it after each procedure in order to sterilize it," complained another.[20]

With user feedback in hand, Thorne quickly reengineered the probe, retaining the crucial nonstick properties but streamlining the design and making it easily sterilizable in a conventional autoclave.* By December

❝One key question loomed. Which of the many surgical specialties should Silverglide target first?❞

1998, the new probe, in five sizes, won FDA approval. It was thinner (for better access to the surgical site) and required no disassembly for sterilization. But one key question loomed: Which of the many surgical specialties should Silverglide target first?

Thorne had heard that sticking tissue was a source of frustration for most surgeons, regardless of their surgical specialty. He decided that a good first market segment to target would be plastic surgeons. Why? First, the appearance of the surgery's outcome was especially important. "Sticking tissue can cause complications that mar the final appearance of the surgical procedure," Thorne pointed out, "so the Silverglide probe should offer significant benefits to this target market. Further, 85 percent of the 9,000 doctors who do plastic surgery do most of their work in their own independent clinics, so they themselves are the decision-makers when it comes to choices among surgical tools and equipment. There's no hospital bureaucracy to wade through in order to make a sale."[21]

Entering the Market

Fortunately for Silverglide, there were a few key trade shows that most plastic surgeons attended each year, to hear the latest research, learn the newest techniques, and learn about new products like the Silverglide probe.

Securing a small booth at one of these shows, Thorne and his cofounder Kevin Morningstar demonstrated the nonstick properties of the Silverglide probe by performing surgery on meat and fresh fish fillets. Though the demonstration didn't

---

*Surgical tools are sterilized after each use in an autoclave (a sterilization chamber involving steam under pressure), so that every surgical procedure is conducted with a sterile set of tools.

smell very good, a few surgeons bought probes on the spot, while others asked for follow-up calls following the show. Two surgical products distributors also agreed to take on the probe and offer it to their surgical clients. Within a few weeks, two surgeons had become excited enough by their surgical results that they agreed to let Silverglide shoot videos of the probe in action and provide testimonials of its effectiveness.

Small Problems, Big Problems

Alas, after four months of dogged effort, progress was proving difficult to come by. There were several stumbling blocks, Thorne reported to his advisory board.

> First, we're a new company that most surgeons have never heard of. Second, to make a sale, we have to convince the surgeon that the probe doesn't stick, and we also have to convince them that a probe itself is a useful surgical tool. It's not one that most of them have used before. Third, for the distributor, there's not much incentive to show our product. It's a very small product line (only probes, in only five sizes), and even if they like it, there's little incentive to reorder, since the probe lasts for hundreds of surgical procedures. It's not clear to the distributors that the sales are going to be enough to be worth their selling time. The educational process is an uphill road.[22]

You read at the outset of this chapter, in Vinod Khosla's words, "If you don't have a big problem, you don't have a big opportunity. Nobody will pay you to solve a non-problem."[23] Thorne was beginning to question whether he was on the right track.

His report continued. There were two key questions to address. First,

A plastic surgeon told me last week that he simply doesn't use probes. He and a number of other surgeons basically said the same thing: "If you can make non-stick forceps, I'll buy them." So maybe forceps are a better way to go. One good thing about forceps is that surgeons need as many as a dozen sizes and shapes of forceps on each surgical tray that they use for each surgical procedure. If a surgeon does two or three procedures a day, that's a lot more sales potential than we seem to have with the probe, where one or two sizes seem to be all a surgeon can use.

"The second question we have to address," said Thorne, "is whether to stay with plastic surgeons as our focus." He continued,

They use forceps, too, as most surgeons do. But there's another target market that could be attractive: neurosurgery. Sticking tissue is a problem in the brain (a few brain cells here or there is really important!) or near the spine, where they do most of their work. Electrosurgical forceps are one of the neurosurgeon's primary instruments. And in hospital settings, where neurosurgeons do most of their work, if there are a typical six operating rooms and two or three procedures per day in each room, plus some backup stock, that's a lot of forceps. Unlike the plastic surgeons who run their own clinics, though, there are lots of chefs in the buying kitchen, so the sale cycle might be a lot longer, and getting through the hospital bureaucracy probably wouldn't be easy.

Changing one's product offering as well as one's target market is a long-odds task, Thorne knew. There would be much to get right, and many things that could go wrong. But, at the end of the day, if the current strategy is not working, something must change, he reasoned. "There is no guarantee that we will be successful in developing a non-stick forceps," he continued. But "I do know that Kevin and I have more knowledge about what makes tissue stick and how to prevent it than virtually anyone else in the world."

❝Thorne discovered that the benefits of nonsticking forceps were even more tangible than he had thought. ❞

It took the better part of a year to get a deal done with a US original equipment manufacturer (OEM) of forceps, to whose instruments Silverglide would apply its nonstick alloy, to raise more money, and to get FDA approval. Along the way, Thorne discovered that the benefits of nonsticking forceps were even more tangible than he had thought. Not only was the doctor's "pain" eliminated, by eliminating the frustration that accompanied the sticking tissue, but doctors could also work considerably faster. This meant that more procedures could be performed in the same amount of time. More procedures meant more money— music to a surgeon's ears! Perhaps he was on to a somewhat bigger customer problem to solve! In June 2000, the new forceps went to market.

At a trade show in the summer of 2000, Dr. Alan Stormo, who had been using an early set of Silverglide prototypes for almost a year and the probe for more than two years, brought a trio of fellow surgeons to the Silverglide booth and asked Thorne to tell his colleagues about the new forceps range. "Are they really nonstick?" asked one. Dr. Stormo provided the answer. "I told you, they just don't stick. On a sticking scale of 1–10, they're a zero."[24] Word spread, and Silverglide's sales finally began to grow.

The Rest of the Story

While the subsequent stages in Silverglide's journey were not always easy, five years later a large global medical instruments company came knocking. It wanted to buy Silverglide and put Thorne's silver alloy technology to use on a wider range of surgical instruments than Silverglide itself had the resources to develop and take to market. Nonstick instruments were in demand, and Silverglide had the best technology. Thorne and his investors agreed to sell the company for a sum that made all of them very happy. Today, as a leading clinician notes on the Silverglide website, "The Silverglide forceps are remarkable. We use them in surgery after surgery without tissue sticking."[25]

Allowing his customers' problems to drive his company's circuitous journey had required adaptability and patience, to be sure. But those attributes, combined with Thorne's problem-first logic and his patented technology, paid off, in spades!

Apex Ski Boots: Is There a Compelling Customer Problem Here?[26]

One sunny summer day in June 2008, entrepreneurs, business partners, and occasional angel investors David Sosnowski and John Murphy finished a round of golf. They adjourned to the clubhouse where they met their long-time friend Denny Hanson, who had a new venture underway. Hanson, a ski industry pioneer who was passionate about boots, had created Hanson Industries back in the 1970s. Hanson boots were notable for their product innovation, including their unique rear-entry form, which made them more comfortable than the more typical front-entry boots.

Although his company eventually went out of business, Hanson never let go of the idea of creating a comfortable but high-performance ski boot. As the popularity of snowboarding took off in the early 2000s, Hanson observed, "Look at those

> **Although his company eventually went out of business, Hanson never let go of the idea of creating a comfortable but high-performance ski boot.**

snowboarders walking around in those comfy warm boots. Why can't we create a ski boot like that?"[27] The idea for Apex Ski Boots was born.

The product-first Apex boot that Hanson envisaged featured a two-piece design. A soft snowboard-like boot would be encased in a carbon-fiber shell with buckles, and would be compatible with standard ski bindings. Hanson's idea was that skiers could walk around in the warmth and comfort of the inner boot, and, when they were ready to hit the slopes, simply step into the outer shell and buckle up.

Sosnowksi and Murphy were among those to whom Hanson had provided early prototypes for testing during the preceding ski season. Sosnowksi was smitten. As he put it, "Who doesn't want a more comfortable ski boot? This is a great product. It's a no brainer."[28] The duo, along with a few of their friends, agreed to finance a production run of 2,000 pairs for the coming ski season, to the tune of $640,000.

Industry Challenges

Alas, by the end of the following ski season, only 1,400 pairs had been sold, and the new company was running short of cash. Over the next eight years, Sosnowski, Murphy, and their fellow investors learned many painful lessons about the business side of skiing that proved far more difficult than they had imagined.

First, the prime selling season was short. "The season starts in late September and runs through the Christmas holidays. Outside that, you won't sell much at all," Murphy soon discovered. The short sales window, along with restrictive terms from the Chinese supplier, created cash flow issues. "You've got to pay the Chinese in June, but you don't get delivery until end of August. September is when you're getting product into the retailers, but they've got tough 60-day payment terms, so we're not getting paid from them until at least November. Then the retailers have aggressive return policies so we may be taking product back a few months later. Cash flow is brutal!" exclaimed Murphy.[29]

Forecasting sales was no easier. "Estimating volumes and sizes to meet demand is extremely difficult. No matter how much analysis you do, you'll always guess wrong on sizes and will end up with excess inventory of some sizes and be short with others," recalled Murphy.[30] The 600 unsold pairs after the 2008–2009 season was a typical amount in the years to follow.

Unpredictable and inconsistent winter weather was another major factor. "If the ski season is bad, then demand goes down, and the weather is always bad somewhere," said Murphy. "We can have great skiing on the East Coast, which will be good for sales there, but a dry season in the Rockies or out West will kill sales in those areas. You just can't predict it."[31]

Even more daunting was the reality that in this product-based business, as Murphy put it,

> Growth eats cash. In our IT services business, growth always produced cash, but that's not the case here. We've learned that lesson the hard way. The more we sell, the more cash we need to prepay for the boots, hold the inventory, and then wait for our retailers to pay us. We simply keep having to put more money in.[32]

Distribution Channel Woes

The most difficult challenges, though, were with the ski shops who sold Apex and other ski boots. "Even if we had the right product in all the right stores at the right time and the conditions were great, we always faced resistance from the boot-fitters in the ski shops. Unless they promote your boot, you won't sell many," said Murphy. Boot-fitters were influential in the sales process and their recommendations were key. The major ski boot brands knew this and they reportedly paid spiffs of $50 or more to the boot-fitter every time he or she sold one of their models. Given its limited cash, Apex was unable to do so. Further, Apex boots carried premium pricing, ranging from $1,000 to $1,200 per pair, which presented another selling challenge.

Moreover, Apex boots caused confusion in the ski shop service departments because the Apex shell was about an inch longer than a traditional boot of the same foot size. The technicians who mounted and adjusted skis required special training on Apex boots so they could mount them according to the ski and binding manufacturer-recommended specifications.

Apex Goes Nowhere

Despite numerous tweaks to the product from time to time, the result of the continuing parade of cash flow and other challenges meant that the investor group had to keep putting more money in, always hoping that the next year would be different. By 2017, despite having changed CEOs in 2014, Murphy and the other angel investors had invested more than $6 million into Apex Ski Boots, which remained unprofitable and cash starved.

Fast-forwarding to the 2021–2022 ski season, Apex was touting its boots as "Pain-free. Performance-driven," and "Ski hard. Walk easy."[33] Its website proclaims, "Our boot system blends the comfort, fit and warmth of a snowboard boot into a revolutionary Open-Chassis™ design that is unlike anything on the market."[34]

❝Perhaps the real issue deterring Apex' progress is a more straightforward one: Exactly what is the problem that Apex boots are seeking to solve?❞

While the industry and distribution channel issues have made Apex's journey a difficult one, other boot makers seem to have been able to manage them. Perhaps the real issue deterring Apex's progress was a more straightforward one: Exactly what is the problem that Apex boots are seeking to solve? Is it walkability? Is it comfort? Is it the cold feet that are part and parcel of this cold-weather sport? In other words, what problem (that matters to its skier customers and its retail partners) does the Apex boot solve better than other boots, and for what kind of skier? Problem-first logic to the rescue, please. Product-first logic simply hasn't worked. Will Apex identify and capture a successful niche in the ski boot market some day? Time will tell.

Lessons About Problem-First versus Product-First Mindsets—and More

Why might one argue that problem-first mindsets are likely to lead to better outcomes than the product-first thinking that we saw from Sosnowski, Murphy, and Hanson? Surely, a handful of case studies is insufficient to definitively prove the case, one way or the other. And other counterexamples abound. In its early days, did Starbucks resolve a customer problem, for example? Arguably, it provided customer delight, an altogether different notion, offering a substantially upgraded customer experience compared to the traditional American coffee shop of the 1970s, albeit at a much higher price. But did American consumers have a "problem" getting a cup of coffee when they were out and about? Probably not. So what are the lessons we might take away from this chapter?

On the benefit of focus: The case studies in this chapter collectively suggest that problem-first mindsets help entrepreneurs focus on a set of customers they seek to serve and thereby get clear about exactly who it is that has the problem. For Phil Knight and Bill Bowerman, it was elite distance runners. For Simon Cohen, it was Mexican importers importing goods from China, a previously untapped market segment. For Jon Thorne, it was plastic surgeons (and later, neurosurgeons). For the Apex Ski Boots team, heaven only knows which skiers they seek to target! Perhaps they don't know!

It is also often the case that, in Jon Thorne's words, "Winning a large share of a narrow target market is easier than winning a small share of a wider market."[35] That's because you can more easily understand that narrow segment's unique problems or needs, as we'll explore more deeply in Chapter 4, and then tailor your product accordingly.

On ascertaining the importance of the problem you seek to solve: This set of case studies also suggests that problem-first thinkers must ascertain the extent to which the supposed problems they are tackling are sufficiently meaningful to encourage their target customers to change their buying behavior—no small feat! Nike's distance runners' problems—shin splints, sprained ankles, and more—were felt viscerally. No question there. Simon Cohen's customers probably slept better knowing the status of their shipments. Silverglide's surgeons' frustrations with sticking tissue proved real. But note that while Jon Thorne's early customers appreciated the nonstick properties of his surgical probe, their more important problems surfaced when they had surgical forceps—not a probe, which few had occasion to use—in hand.

But Apex? How important is it for skiers to be able to walk easily in their ski boots (presumably while also having to carry the outer shell of an Apex boot with them)? And what about comfort? Are most ski boots really uncomfortable and pain-inducing, given the advances that boot makers have made in the past couple of decades? And what about cold feet? Apex and its investors might have benefited from some well-crafted marketing research to ascertain the degree to which the walkability and comfort "problems" were real, and by whom they were felt. Alas, there was no such evidence, only supposition. Attempting to build a successful entrepreneurial venture on the back of somebody's hunches is risky, indeed!

Bonus Lessons Learned

This chapter has delivered a couple of important lessons to enable you to make product-first logic an integral part of *your* entrepreneurial mindset. But that's not all we can learn here. There are additional lessons, too, as one might expect from the likes of Phil Knight, Simon Cohen, and Jon Thorne.

On the value of early learning: The Nike case study shows us that the hands-on tactical lessons learned from building a highly focused business serving one market segment can create a foundation on which an entrepreneur can build additional entries into other segments, by employing the same principles. What Nike learned about designing shoes to meet specific sports' needs, about sourcing shoes from Asian manufacturers, and about how to win endorsements from athletes and build high-impact marketing on their coattails served it well as it grew beyond the running shoe segment.

On the likelihood of having to pivot: Silverglide's Jon Thorne learned that having a proprietary technology that solved a real problem—sticking tissue—was a perhaps necessary but insufficient ingredient in building a successful company. Doing so at Silverglide meant pivoting away from the surgical probe toward another surgical instrument, bipolar forceps, that was the bread-and-butter tool of choice for many surgeons. In my experience, it takes a pivot or two—sometimes more!—to match a new technology with an appropriate and genuine customer problem. When Max Levchin sought to put his world-class encryption skills to work to build the company we now know as PayPal, it was Plan G, the seventh application of that technology, that provided a way forward.[36] Levchin's Plans A through F did not pan out.

Silverglide's success with its nonstick forceps also provided a platform for creating other nonstick electrosurgical instruments that its acquirer valued. Sometimes, the future value of the business you build will be realized by others. But if they can see that potential, they will pay you for it!

On going the extra mile for your customer: The Simon Cohen story also points out the value of going the extra mile for your customer, even if that means awakening at 2 a.m. each morning or losing money on a particular transaction when things go awry. Not only did Cohen himself engage in such behavior, but by doing so he set an example that his employees were expected to emulate.[37] Such highly visible examples, or artifacts, are a key element in how strong cultures like CMN's are built.[38]

On getting the business model right, too: The Silverglide story shows us that even using a problem-first mindset to get the product right, the use case right, and to uncover the right target customer involves more than determining whether the product is valued by customers. It's equally important, perhaps more important, that the business model with which those customers are to be served is a viable one, and that the overall opportunity is sufficiently attractive. For Silverglide, the fact that bipolar forceps existed in a wide variety of sizes and shapes, and were used in virtually every surgical procedure, meant that hospitals would need to buy them in substantial quantities, thereby making the cost of securing such customers affordable.

In my view, while getting the product right via a problem-first mindset is crucially important for any entrepreneur, too many aspiring entrepreneurs—and too many marketers in large businesses—stop there and fail to consider other issues that are important to long-run success. Is the market attractive? Is the industry one in which I'd like to (and have a chance to successfully) compete? Have I assembled the right team to pursue this particular opportunity?[39] For Apex, the daunting cash-flow characteristics of that industry as well as the other industry challenges made survival and growth particularly hard to achieve.

How to Add "Problem-First, Not Product-First, Logic" to *Your* Entrepreneurial Mindset

"Okay, I get it, John," you say. "But what can I do now to find a worthwhile problem I or my team can solve?" Whether you're an aspiring entrepreneur or a big-business type hoping or helping your company to think and act more counter-conventionally and break some rules, here's a start.

Make a bug list: Every minute of every day, we come into contact with people and situations, some of which somehow seem suboptimal. When I first moved to the United Kingdom more than 20 years ago, I wondered why most bathroom sinks had separate spigots for hot water and cold water. Why not let mixed hot and cold water—adjusted to just the right temperature—be mixed within the faucet instead of in the bowl?

My advice is that you carry with you a notepad (or use an app on your phone) and make note of everything you encounter that "bugs you"—that is, could be done better. Maybe the step is too high getting on the bus you ride to work. Maybe there's a system or process at work that's not really getting the job done or not aligning with your company's values. And so on.

If you get yourself into the habit of observing what's around you that could be bettered, you'll soon find an opportunity, I'll wager, about which you really care and for which the skills and capabilities that you bring to the table are particularly, perhaps uniquely, well suited.

Sort the problems categorically: Our lives, at least for most of us, can be divided into different buckets or categories, in various ways: Work vs. leisure. Activities we do solo vs. those we do with others. Family vs. friends, sports vs. music, and so on. Once each month, look at your bug list and sort it into categories that are meaningful to you. Doing so is likely to stimulate your curiosity. It will also give you clues about where your interests lie and perhaps connect some dots among them.

Only then, imagine alternative solutions: At the end of the day, you'll need not only to identify problems to solve for some set of customers, but you'll also need to provide solutions they will buy. I suggest that each month, you choose one or two of the problems you've identified and imagine as many alternative ways to solve them as you can. An app? A service? A product? Perhaps engage your friends or fellow employees in doing so. Training your mind to seek alternatives, instead of jumping at the first solution you identify, will enhance your creativity and serve you well.

Closing Thoughts

There you have it: a case for adopting a problem-first, rather than a product-first mindset in building your business, whether in a new venture or on a path you are already traveling—plus some steps you can take now to make *your* mindset more entrepreneurial and break the typical product-first rule. While Vinod Khosla's observation that "Nobody will pay you to solve a nonproblem" is not the only way forward, as the Starbucks example illustrates, it's a helpful idea to keep you focused on your customer, as we saw with Simon Cohen. Solve a real and meaningful problem for your customers, serve them well, and you're likely to be well on your way to eventual success!

4

Why "Moving the Needle" Doesn't Matter Much to Entrepreneurs: Think Narrow, Not Broad

In most well-established companies, there are processes for just about everything, and for good reason. Good processes drive both efficiency and effectiveness. They help people do their jobs more easily. They help deliver results.

When it comes to new product development, there's a process for that, too. Drawing on the seminal work of Robert Cooper,[1] it's become the norm that ideas for new products are put thorough a series of "gates" through which they must pass in order to qualify for launch. At each of the gates, a "go" or "no-go" decision is reached that permits the project to proceed to the next stage in the process or be killed.

In essence, this conventional process is intended to ensure that the proposed product or service, if launched, will meet the company's targets in terms of revenue, market share, return on investment, profitability, or some other relevant metrics. In other words, will it "move the needle" and contribute meaningfully to the company's growth and profit objectives.

In spite of the widespread use of such stage-gate processes, however, Hanover Research, a consultancy that helps companies manage and implement them, reports that "Almost half of new products launched will fail within the first year."[2] The high failure rate of new products is testament to the difficulty entailed in understanding what customers want or need and developing solutions they will buy. Could it be that seeking to play in markets that can "move the needle" is a rule worth breaking?

Entrepreneurs need neither stages nor gates: In Chapter 3, you saw how Phil Knight and Bill Bowerman created Nike by focusing on distance runners' problems: their need for more cushioning and better lateral stability in their running shoes. But Knight and Bowerman did something else well, too. They focused at the outset on an extremely narrow target market: elite distance runners in the Western United States, those who could run nearly a four-minute mile. If there was ever a competition for the narrowest target market, this one might win!

While large process-driven companies are applying stage-gate methodology to determine whether a new product idea will be substantial enough to "move the needle," many entrepreneurs adopt an entirely different mindset. They find a *very* narrow target market whose unique needs or problems they know and understand intimately, and they set out to address those needs or problems, with little regard for how large the opportunity actually is. They figure that once they've built success in serving the initial (albeit small) market, they will have learned some things that will enable them to move on to adjacent market segments or develop additional products for the segment in which they started.

This mindset—thinking narrowly, not broadly—is exactly where Knight and Bowerman began their journey, which eventually exceeded almost anyone's wildest expectations. Think narrowly at the outset, learn as you go, and a broader market is likely to eventually come your way.

What's ahead in Chapter 4: In this chapter, we'll start by examining the story of Nespresso, the originator of barista-quality single-serve espresso that can be prepared and consumed at home. Surprisingly, as we'll see, this is a story that played out within a large multinational company, not in an entrepreneur's garage.

> **Surprisingly, as we'll see, this is a story that played out within a large multinational company, not in an entrepreneur's garage.**

Next, we'll study Pandora, today's leading global maker of affordable jewelry, which also built its stunning success around thinking narrowly, not broadly. Who would have guessed that selling charm bracelets could become a multibillion-dollar business? We'll wrap up the case studies with the story of a business in Tunisia, Visual Optical, that started its journey ambitiously and broadly, with unfortunate consequences. Sometimes the best teacher is failure.

Then to close the chapter, as always, we'll examine the lessons that these case studies deliver—for thinking narrowly, not broadly, and some bonus lessons, too. Finally, whether you're in a business large or small, new or long established, you'll get some pragmatic next steps you can take now to make "think narrow" a part of *your* entrepreneurial mindset. Here we go!

Nespresso: Will Single-Serve Coffee Capsules "Move the Needle"?

In the mid-1970s, Nestlé was the global leader in instant coffee, with its Nescafé brand the runaway best-seller in a category that accounted for 30 percent of global coffee sales. A Swiss engineer in Nestlé's packaging department, Éric Favre, was tired of his Italian wife's teasing that the Swiss knew nothing about coffee. He and Anna Maria decided that a vacation in Italy was in order, so that she could educate her husband about what real coffee tasted like.

Exploring the cafes in Rome, the couple discovered one, the Caffè Sant'Eustachio, with a much longer queue of coffee enthusiasts than others, all queueing up for espresso. A barista named Eugenio told them the secret. He and his fellow baristas aerated the coffee by pulling the lever not just once, but at several short intervals. "It's chemistry: oxidation brings out all the flavours and aromas," Favre later explained.[3] Infatuated, Favre decided to figure out how to build a machine that would replicate Eugenio's process and brew espresso of which Anna-Maria would be proud.

Back home in Switzerland, Favre began tinkering in his free time. But Nestlé wasn't interested. Eventually, Nestlé's food service division saw that Favre's invention—a machine that pumped pressurised water through small capsules of ground coffee, delivering an attractive and tasty cup of espresso with the requisite *crema* on top—might help it penetrate the restaurant market. In 1982, however, following a disappointing test in eight Swiss restaurants, the restaurant strategy was abandoned, and the focus became the office market.

In 1986, with the office market not working out either, the business was moved outside of Nestlé's headquarters, "so that it could establish credibility and so that it didn't have to fight against all the company's rules," recalled Camillo Pagano, a senior vice president. Manufacturing of the machines was outsourced to a kitchen appliance maker, and a production line was set up to make the capsules. But by the end of 1987, only half the machines that had been manufactured had been sold, and the maker of the machines was not happy. Without machines, of course, capsules could not be sold. The project was floundering.

Changing of the Guard

In 1988, in a rare move for Nestlé, which almost always promoted people from within, an outsider was brought in to figure out what to do with Nespresso. Jean-Paul Gaillard had built a dramatically successful line of Marlboro Classics clothing for Philip Morris, a tobacco company and the purveyor of Marlboro cigarettes. Working alongside Favre, he quickly tore up the former strategy. "At the original launch, the product was wrong, the positioning was wrong, and the targeting was wrong. It had cost a lot of money and brought nothing," he recalled.[4]

Observing the emergence and early growth of Starbucks in the United States and others like it in the United Kingdom and Europe, Gaillard decided to change the focus and target individual upscale coffee drinkers, figuring that consumers learning to enjoy espresso might like to make it at home. "I wanted to create the Chanel of coffee and decided to make Nespresso chic and bobo. The idea was to keep it to the level of people who have a doorman."[5] A narrow market? Absolutely!

Problems Arise—and a Solution, Too

Before long, product reliability complaints began to appear with the Nespresso machines. Gaillard knew that quick service turnaround was essential, but Nestlé was neither manufacturing nor servicing the machines. Turning this technical issue into a marketing asset, he launched the Nespresso Club in 1989. Anyone buying a machine or ordering capsules was automatically enrolled. The club offered Nespresso's discerning customers three things:

- 24/7 order-taking for capsules for delivery within two business days
- Prompt handling of service calls
- Personalized advice from coffee experts

The Nespresso Club, the first direct marketing effort within the entire Nestlé organization, gave the entire Nespresso experience a feeling of exclusivity. Customers were required to provide their names, mailing

" The Nespresso Club, the first direct marketing effort within the entire Nestlé organization, gave the entire Nespresso experience a feeling of exclusivity. "

addresses, and email addresses. The club grew quickly. By the end of 1990, there were 2,700 members spread across Switzerland, France, Japan, and the United States. Germany and the Benelux countries were added in 1992, followed by Spain, Austria, and the United Kingdom in 1996. By 1997, the club had grown to 220,000 members and the business had turned the corner to breakeven.[6]

The Nespresso Club was not Gaillard's only means of establishing exclusivity for his now fast-growing brand. He restricted sales of pods and machines to only a few select avenues: Nespresso boutiques, the online Nespresso store, and a few select upscale retail stores like Harrods in London. The Nespresso boutiques weren't on every street corner either. They were placed only in exclusive shopping areas like the Champs Elysée in Paris and the upscale Knightsbridge shopping district in London.

The patented machines, initially manufactured in Italy by a sole supplier, were licensed to the likes of Krups and Alessi, upscale kitchen appliance brands that not only gave the machines additional cachet but also paved the way for further penetration into the best retail outlets.

A Maverick Moves On

As the business grew, it became clear that Gaillard was the driving force who had turned Favre's technical invention into a marketable product. But Gaillard was no ordinary man-

> **When Nestlé's structure got in the way of the rapid innovation he wanted, he rejected it.**

ager. He was forceful in pushing his ideas with Nestlé top management and relished the challenges when they pushed back. He recruited young talent from the top consumer goods brands and encouraged them to take risks, breaking Nestlé's "rules" where necessary. When Nestlé's structure got in the way of the rapid innovation he wanted, he rejected it. At one point, he was so confident of Nespresso's potential that he offered to buy the business from Nestlé.[7] Gaillard left Nespresso in 1997, at which point Nespresso was turning over SFr150 million in revenue annually.

Nespresso after Gaillard

A long-time Nestlé insider took the reins as Nespresso's new CEO, with an agreed goal of turning the brand into a SFr1 billion business over the next 10 years. At that size, in the words of Nestlé's CEO Peter Brabeck-Letmathe, it would then become "an interesting business for a company the size of Nestlé."[8] Nespresso was still not "moving the needle" for Nestlé after a 15-year journey! But eventually it would, and then some, hitting the SFr3 billion mark in 2010.[9] It had become Nestle's fastest growing brand.[10]

And what about Gaillard, you might wonder? As Nestlé's patents began to expire, in 2008 Gaillard founded the Ethical Coffee Company to produce biodegradable coffee capsules that were compatible with Nespresso's machines. Over the next 10 years, in his words, his company and others "turned the single-serve coffee market from a monopoly into a free market, resulting in the fastest growing segment in the F&B [food and beverage] sector."[11] Thinking narrowly, still!

Pandora's Rocket Ship Ride[12]

In 1982, a Danish goldsmith named Per Enevoldsen and his wife, Winnie, opened a small jewelry shop in Copenhagen. Most days Winnie could be found serving customers while Per worked on crafting new designs. They routinely traveled to Thailand to source materials and to find attractive styles to import. Why Thailand? "The craftmanship in Thailand is incredible," Enevoldsen remarked to Winnie after one of their trips. "We can buy these designs and sell them at lower prices than our competitors."[13]

Not entirely satisfied with the customer traffic their store was getting, the couple decided that wholesaling might offer a better opportunity. That business began to flourish, and in 1987, they closed the store to focus on wholesaling, selling both their locally made as well as imported jewelry to Danish retailers. In 1989, the couple moved to Thailand and set up a small 10-person manufacturing facility near Bangkok. Enevoldsen decided to focus his own efforts on the manufacturing operation and hired a Danish designer, Lone Frandsen, to create new designs. Kenneth Ramstrup, a trusted friend, also came on board in Denmark to take over the sales role.

Thanks to Frandsen's unique designs, the low cost of production in Thailand, and Ramstrup's sales prowess, the business grew modestly but steadily. In 1996, a second designer, Lisbeth Larsen, joined the team. By 1999, Ramstrup had won nearly 200 jewelry-store customers across Scandinavia and annual revenues were approaching the DKK800 million mark about £1 million. It was a successful but modest business by any account.

Narrowing the Focus

In the summer of 1999, Ramstrup discovered that an Italian jewelry company had won an award for a charm bracelet that was unlike any other. Unlike most other charm bracelets, on which gravity would force all of the charms to drop to the lowest point on the bracelet, the Italian bracelet was constructed in such a way that the charms stayed in place. "We could do this!" he exclaimed to the team.[14] Frandsen and Larsen loved the idea.

> Charms can tell the story of your life: your wedding, your children's births, your special holidays, your milestone birthdays, even Valentine's Day and Christmas. They can be very affordable or rather expensive. The possibilities are endless![15]

Enevoldsen, Frandsen, and Larsen got to work, eventually developing and patenting a silver bracelet that allowed charms to be threaded onto the bracelet and spaced precisely. The idea was that the bracelet and about 20 charms would be offered to the company's retailers in an elegant box—"It's Pandora's box!" suggested a part-time employee,[16] thereby unknowingly giving the company the new name that would one day become a global brand.

Ramstrup took the first boxes to a few of his customers in 2000, asking them to display them on their counters. Soon, shop assistants were telling their customers about the charms they had bought, and what each charm meant to them. Customers would buy a bracelet and a few charms, then come back for more. Sales took off. The Pandora jewelry was turning over in 16 days, dramatically faster than the industry's six-month norm![17]

Word of Pandora's hot-selling new charm bracelet began to spread. Michael Lund Peterson, a Dane living in the United States, asked for and won the rights to the US market in 2003. By the end of 2004, he'd secured 700 jewelry store accounts, a number that doubled in 2005.[18] Germany and Australia quickly followed.

Meanwhile, Winnie was managing the growing company's finances. Happily, Pandora was profitable and generating plenty of cash, thanks to the highly efficient manufacturing system that her husband had put in place and the tight control that Ramstrup exercised over his distributors, which reliably paid their invoices on time. Enevoldsen was ramping up production, thanks to a new five-story facility he'd opened in 2005 in Gemopolis, a free trade zone near Bangkok. Inventory was being shipped as fast as the Thai workforce could produce it.

Winnie's Worry

By 2006, Pandora jewelry was being sold in 20 countries. Revenues were doubling each year. Its single hit product, the charm bracelet, accounted for some 90 percent of sales![19] It looked like 2007 sales could surpass £100 million, if all went well. Ramstrup was spending much of his time explaining to his retail accounts why they couldn't have as much Pandora product as they wanted, as production was struggling to meet the rapidly growing demand. But Winnie was worried. "The Italian charm bracelet has apparently peaked and we're told that its sales have slipped. What if that happens to Pandora? This might just be a fad and demand could fall any day."[20]

> **❝Its single hit product, the charm bracelet, accounted for some 90 percent of sales!❞**

Beyond Winnie's worries was the unspoken fact that the entire Pandora team was feeling stretched to the breaking point. No one had imagined in their wildest dreams that a single product line—the charm bracelet and all its charms—could catapult Pandora from a very modest start to DKK1 billion in sales in seven short years. "We're doing well," counseled Enevoldsen. "We just need more people and structure."[21] It was decided that hiring an experienced CEO was the best way to proceed.

Strengthening the Team

In March 2007, the search, led by Ramstrup and Martin Hoyer-Hansen, an external advisor, got underway. An attractive candidate who had run Denmark for Zara, the fast-growing European fast-fashion retailer, was interested. Once he discovered the high volumes that Pandora was doing and its phenomenal rate of growth, he came back with a private equity investor in tow. Hoyer-Hansen liked the idea. "I'm not sure that a CEO alone will solve all your problems," he said to Enevoldsen. "A private equity firm will take a lot of the difficulties off your plate very quickly."[22]

Negotiations ensued. Alas, in August 2007, the deal fell through, as the Danish investor was unable to sell the deal to their Swedish partners. The ex-Zara candidate then came back with two other private equity firms. One was quickly rejected; the other soon pulled out, giving five reasons for backing out of the deal. Among them were concerns over Pandora's reliance on a single product, the charm bracelet; limited success with past launches of other Pandora products; and the risk that it was all a fad. Though everyone at Pandora was by now exhausted, partly due to the ever-expanding workload and partly due to the emotional rollercoaster of deals appearing imminent, then falling out, by early November, three interested private equity firms were identified. It was agreed up front that any deal would have to value Pandora at not less than DKK3 billion (about £300 million).[23]

Harvesting the Value That Thinking Narrowly Had Created

In 2008, Axcel, a Danish private equity firm, bought a 60 percent stake from the Enevoldsens and other shareholders for a reported DKK 2.4 billion, valuing the business at DKK 4 billion (about £400 million).[24] Two years later, in October 2010, the business was listed on the NASDAQ OMX Copenhagen Stock Exchange, selling US$1.83 billion worth of shares, nearly DKK10 billion, on its first day. At the end of the day, the listing gave Pandora, which had become the world's third largest jewelry company behind only Cartier and Tiffany, a market capitalization of some

DKK27 billion (nearly £3 billion, 10 times the valuation Pandora had been seeking just three years earlier).[25] Pandora had truly gone global, with its products available in more than 10,000 outlets in more than 55 countries.[26] A short-lived fad? Not!

Thinking narrowly, not broadly, with a laser-like focus on charm bracelets, had provided the Enevoldsens, their early employees, their distributors who'd become shareholders, and their private equity backers with astonishing returns! Is there a break-the-rules lesson here? Thinking narrowly might serve you well, too!

The Visual Optical Team Thinks (Too) Broadly[27]

In 1998, the venture capital and private equity industry in Tunisia was in its early days. Deal flow was scarce. In order to make suitable investments, Aziz Mebarek, Karim Trad, and their partners at Tuninvest, one of the country's first private equity firms, had to seek out companies that had the potential to grow. They would then try to convince the founders that, with Tuninvest's help (and cash!) they could grow much faster—and make money for themselves and for Tuninvest, too.

In 1998, Mebarek and Trad identified just such an opportunity. After earning an optician's diploma in Brussels and after working in Germany for one of the world leaders in optical technology, Mondher M'Henni had returned to his homeland and opened an optical shop in Sousse, a small city 100 miles from the country's capital, Tunis.

M'Henni, an ambitious fellow and a gifted salesperson, soon saw that he could expand his business by securing the exclusive rights to import sunglasses and eyeglass frames from some of the world's leading fashion brands, including Police, Sting, Fendi, and Dolce & Gabbana. By 1998 he was running a small but thriving business that consisted of three elements:

1. Retailing: Selling eyeglasses and sunglasses to consumers in Sousse and in a second shop he'd opened in Tunis.
2. Wholesaling: Importing eyeglass frames and sunglasses and selling them to other opticians throughout Tunisia, of which there were approximately 150.
3. Manufacturing: M'Henni had set up a factory to manufacture glass lenses for eyeglasses sold in his shop and to other opticians.

Intrigued by the potential he saw in M'Henni and his business, Tuninvest's Trad suggested to M'Henni that together they could open and grow a chain of optical shops similar to the chains that were growing rapidly in France and elsewhere in Europe, and to continue to develop the wholesaling and manufacturing activities, too.

Getting Underway

Trad was excited about proceeding with an investment in Visual Optical. "The market is attractive, with promising trends and plenty of room for further development. And improved operations management is something we should be able to bring to the company."[28]

But that was not all he liked. The activities of the company, though diverse, were complementary, and the portfolio of brands was strong and performing well. The company was financially healthy, which came as no surprise, given the new Mercedes that M'Henni was driving and his posh home in one of Tunis's most affluent suburbs. The cash flow generated by the three synergistic lines of business, he reasoned, could help finance the further development of the business, thereby limiting the capital that Tuninvest would have to deploy.

The plan was to open a chain of optical shops as the core of the business, while developing the wholesaling and manufacturing elements alongside. The concept would be in the form of "assisted self-service." "This concept is working in France," observed Trad. "There's no reason it shouldn't work here."[29] The objectives were threefold:

1. They would open two to three new shops each year, each of 150 to 200 square meters.
2. The shops would provide an appealing and comfortable space and a diverse choice of eyewear.
3. Customer service would be the best and most trusted in the market.

Growing the wholesaling business at the same time, Trad reasoned, would also increase the company's clout with its suppliers and enhance the potential for acquiring rights to additional foreign brands. And manufacturing lenses would bring additional profit to the overall bottom line.

To move things along, Tuninvest hired Riyadh Akrout to help M'Henni start implementing the plan. An experienced banker, aged 31, Akrout had been educated abroad and had spent six years managing corporate accounts at Citibank in Tunis, where he had worked with one of Tuninvest's partners. He was a trusted hand. Trad thought Akrout would be the perfect person to complement M'Henni's entrepreneurial spirit.

Things Get Rocky

Alas, it soon became apparent that Akrout and M'Henni would be unable to work together. M'Henni, in Akrout's view, was "a very particular guy who was not amenable to better corporate governance and who wanted to do things his way."[30] M'Henni also found it difficult to work with Akrout and his new investors, who had purchased 80 percent of his company (not including the original shop in Sousse) for 2 million dinars ($1.5 million). They seemed to require "more corporate governance, more accountability and transparency, and a more structured decision-making process,"[31] none of which he was accustomed to. To his astonishment, his new partners were also insisting that all transactions be properly invoiced, and all taxes paid in full! That was not how business was typically done!

Despite the friction, Akrout energetically dove in, hiring new staff, putting new systems in place, and winning some new brands for the portfolio including Gant, Guess, and Elizabeth Arden. But in April, M'Henni decided to step down. He and Akrout agreed that they simply couldn't work together any longer. M'Henni would retain his 20 percent stake, per the original transaction, and become a silent shareholder.

When the 1999 year ended, the financial picture was not pretty. All the changes had cost money and the loss for the year totaled 254,000 dinars ($192,000). Combined revenues were off sharply. Worse, the company's debt had ballooned from 208,000 dinars in December 1998 to a total of 2.2 million dinars ($1.6 million) in December 1999.

But Akrout remained optimistic about Visual Optical's future. "It has been tough. We haven't sold any lenses this year and we have lost some money. M'Henni has left. But we have now consolidated the business, restructured every activity, referenced all our stock, and we now have a clear plan and hopefully no more surprises. Our perspective on the market is still very positive and the year 2000 will be ours."[32]

From Bad to Worse

The new year started well. "We saw some lights at the end of the dark tunnel,"[33] recalled Akrout. The company opened its second retail outlet, doubling its retail presence in Tunis. In March 2000, Akrout inked a joint venture deal with Lynx Optique to develop a retail network of franchised optical outlets in Tunisia. Lynx, a major player in the European optical landscape, managed 120 optical shops in France plus one in Morocco and one in Poland. Visual Optical needed to build a brand, and in Akrout's view, Lynx was the answer.

Alas, as Akrout and his team began remodeling the two shops in Tunis into Lynx franchises, a strong lobby of opticians interfered. The other opticians were not about to let a deep-pocketed financier into the optical game. Wary of losing their high profit margins, they physically blocked Akrout's team from putting up Lynx signs. This practice was not compliant with the current regulations, they claimed.

> **Worse, on the distribution side of the business, with more than a year of history now under his belt, Akrout realized that the inventory simply was not selling.**

Worse, on the distribution side of the business, with more than a year of history now under his belt, Akrout realized that the inventory simply was not selling. Of the initial purchase price, about 1.6 million dinars had been spent on the inventory of sunglasses and frames from prior collections. A reputable accounting firm had done an audit, but its auditor had no idea about the salability of the products. The inventory valuation had simply been wrong. It was clear that a large inventory write-off was required.

With the company's bank overdrafts stretched to their limits and with more cash needed to buy fresh inventory, Tuninvest injected an additional 1.95 million dinars ($1.5 million) in mid-2000. By year-end, however, more bad news arrived: another loss to the tune of nearly 1.5 million dinars ($1.1 million) across the businesses, nearly six times more than the previous year.

Stopping the Bleeding

The 2001 performance was no better, with the loss for the year up to 1.9 million dinars ($1.4 million), largely due to a substantial write-off of inventory (again!) and some delinquent debtors, too. Some opticians, perhaps not surprisingly, were not paying their bills! Finally, after four years of struggle, 2002 results were brighter, with losses having fallen to less than 570,000 dinars ($430,000), thanks in part to a new location within Tunis's first Carrefour store. The retailing business had turned profitable, but more cash was needed to open additional outlets and to buy new frames and sunglasses for the coming season, with import duties due to be paid on arrival.

On the manufacturing side, more capital was required to replace old machinery with new equipment to make plastic lenses, which had become the trend. On top of these needs, the business was burning 15,000 dinars ($11,000) a month, so the additional cash was not going to come from cash flow.

In early 2003, Trad and his partners huddled to decide what to do about Visual Optical. There were several options going forward. One was to invest another million or more dinars to enable the business to carry out its plans and build on its success in the Carrefour location. Another was to sell the manufacturing business and focus on distribution and retailing, which would simplify the business to some degree. But Trad had made a discreet inquiry into selling the manufacturing equipment to SIVO, a lens-maker competitor, which was contemplating an expansion into neighboring Algeria. "Your equipment is worthless," was the reply.

Trad had also inquired about selling Visual Optical's rights to some of its branded imports to another importer. But it quickly became clear that no one would pay for them. Another, but not entirely attractive, option was to sell the business back to M'Henni, whose shop in Sousse was doing well, it seemed. M'Henni had indicated his interest in repurchasing the 80 percent of the business he did not own, but how much he would be willing to pay was unclear.

Tired of losing money year after year, the Tuninvest partners decided to pull the plug. "We had been throwing good money after bad. We had to stop the bleeding,"[34] recalled Trad. The price M'Henni paid, you ask? One dinar. His terms? Clean up the balance sheet and pay off the debt. Total cost to Tuninvest to get out of the deal? Another 600,000 dinars ($450,000). Implications for Mondher M'Henni?

- 2 million dinars still in his pocket from the original deal
- Driving an even fancier car
- Bought back a new business for nothing that had received 2 million dinars of additional investment
- New IT systems
- A new factory closer to Tunis
- And a clean balance sheet, too

If you're leading a slow-growing business, might it lack focus?

If you're planning a start-up, do you want to think broadly and try to do too much? If you're leading a slow-growing business, might it lack focus? In my experience, many such businesses do. The three businesses that Trad and Akrout attempted to build—retailing, frame and sunglasses wholesaling, and lens manufacturing—were complementary in some sense. But they required different sets of skills and capabilities. In light of Visual Optical's rocky journey, you might want to consider narrowing *your* focus, too.

Lessons About Thinking Narrowly, Thinking Broadly—and More

Words like *efficiency, synergy, complementarity*, and the like appear frequently in new product or new business proposals within large and well-established companies. We saw that kind of thinking in Tuninvest, too, as Karim Trad conducted and considered the outcomes of his due diligence on the Visual Optical opportunity in Tunisia.

Nespresso's Jean-Paul Gaillard, Nike's Phil Knight, and Pandora's Per Enevoldsen, however, would have none of that kind of thinking. All three of them thought differently—and narrowly—each in a different way. Nespresso, once Gaillard came on board, would target a *narrow market*, "households who have a doorman," as he put it. For Nike, the narrow target market was elite distance runners. Pandora, following Kenneth Ramstrup's discovery of the Italian charm bracelet, would develop a *narrow product line*—a patented, unique charm bracelet and charms to go with it.

Clearly, entrepreneurial mindsets can exist—and sometimes thrive—in established companies, which both Nestlé and Pandora (née Populair Jewelry) were at the time! So what are the lessons we can learn from how this chapter's case studies broke the "move the needle" rule?

On the power of focus: Focusing narrowly, whether on a narrow *market* or a narrow *product line*, brings important benefits. Whether for entrepreneurs writing their first business plan or those toiling inside a large company, these benefits can be material. They:

- Limit the resources—human, financial, and otherwise— required to move forward
- Aid in understanding the target market's unique and perhaps unmet wants and needs
- Enhance speed to market
- Get everyone rowing the boat in the same direction

Gaillard and Enevoldsen (and Nike's Knight and Bowerman, too) understood this principle. Trad and his partners did not (though they now do—a lesson learned!).[35]

On the reality of "Plan B": Experienced entrepreneurs and experienced early-stage investors know that, most of the time, the "Plan A" so passionately articulated in every pitch deck or new product proposal doesn't work out exactly as planned.

Nespresso's initial forays into the restaurant and office markets didn't pan out. Pandora's original retail shop in a Copenhagen suburb didn't meet the Enevoldsens' goals. Visual Optical stayed the course with their three-pronged approach to the optical market in Tunisia, with very disappointing results. Had they pivoted to just retailing, or just wholesaling, perhaps the outcome would have been better. They and we will never know. But thinking more narrowly might well have improved their odds for success.

❝Wouldn't it be better, some wonder, to have several irons in the fire?❞

One might reasonably ask, though, about the risk entailed in adopting a narrow focus, when that initial focus probably isn't going to work. Wouldn't it be better, some wonder, to have several irons in the fire? For the reasons mentioned earlier, my answer is, "No!" You'll probably have to pivot, perhaps more than once, but a preponderance of evidence suggests that pivoting to a new area of focus is much better than lacking focus at the start.[36]

On the value of outsourcing: Among Jean-Paul Gaillard's first decisions was to outsource the manufacturing of Nespresso machines to kitchen appliance makers. He knew that the real challenge was a marketing challenge. Somebody else could make the machines. In a similar vein, once Pandora discovered that it had a tiger by the tail, it appointed national distributors to take on the challenge of building distribution outside Denmark. Doing so involved capabilities and relationships that Pandora lacked. It's good advice. In building your next venture, think narrowly about what's crucial to do yourself and outsource the rest. Doing so will give you the bandwidth to continuously examine and deepen your understanding of what your narrow target market needs and what your narrow product line should consist of.

On the "large market trap": It's easy to become beguiled by large and potentially attractive markets, as Tuninvest was. Nespresso, too, in its early days, eyeing the 70 percent of the coffee market served by roasted and ground coffee that it did not sell.

"If I can only sell my widget to 1 percent of the people in China, I'll be rich," some say. Market size is important, of course, as there's more room in large markets for multiple companies to be successful. But, as a starting point, I'll take a very narrow target market having a compelling problem that I can solve, and solve better than anyone else. My advice: think narrow at the outset. Moving the needle can come later, once progress is in hand.

On entrepreneurial teams: We saw in Chapter 2 how Amazon's Jeff Bezos and SubWay Link's Arnold Correia went out and found the talent that was required to pursue their dreams. We've seen that pattern again here. Nespresso needed to complement Éric Favre's technical excellence with some marketing savvy. Enter Jean-Paul Gaillard. Visual Optical, on the other hand, hired a trusted person in Riadh Akrout. Trust matters, of course. But Akrout was a banker arguably lacking the skills and capabilities to operate a retailing, wholesaling, and manufacturing business.[37] Granted, skills and capabilities are hard to come by in many labor markets. That's another reason for adopting a narrow focus. Finding suitable and trusted talent that could manage all of what Tuninvest set out to accomplish with Visual Optical was probably nigh on impossible!

Bonus Lessons Learned

From this chapter, like the previous two, you've just read a series of actionable takeaways that are now in hand. They're intended to encourage you to think narrowly, not broadly, about whom you will target and what you will offer them. You can apply those takeaways now *and* in the future, and bake "think narrow, not broad" into the actions you take and the decisions you make. But there's more to learn here.

On the value of patience and perseverance: We saw in Chapter 3 how it took Nike's Phil Knight five years before he was earning enough income to quit his day job as a chartered accountant. It took Nestlé 15 years for CEO Peter Brabeck-Letmathe to observe that Nespresso was finally within striking distance of being a meaningful contributor to Nestlé's bottom line—and it took several more years to actually get there. Per and Winnie Enevoldsen had been in business for 18 years before they discovered the magic of the charm bracelet!

These days, it seems, entrepreneurs are in a great hurry. They want to grow their companies into unicorns the day after tomorrow! But entrepreneurship played to win is typically a long game. Building successful companies for the long term requires a combination of patience and perseverance to stay the course, along with the flexibility to pivot when the data calls for a pivot. It's a journey not for the faint of heart, as we've seen. My advice? Don't rush it. If you're on a sound path, success will come, as Pandora found. If it's a narrow path at the outset, so much the better, as you'll better understand what your narrowly targeted market really wants. One entrepreneur I know well says that entrepreneurship is the art of staying alive until you get lucky! The Pandora story bears that out.

On getting your business model right: Nespresso's Gaillard saw how important it would be to deliver high gross margins on the capsules, given his narrow target market; he priced them accordingly. Gillette does the same in pricing its razor blades. HP, too, with their ink cartridges. On the other hand, the Tuninvest team failed to understand that, if they paid all the requisite taxes, which most of their competitors did not pay, they would be rendered noncompetitive instantly. It's no wonder they struggled from the get-go.

In my experience, focusing on a narrow target market forces entrepreneurs and other innovators to think critically about how their business model will actually work, especially when making pricing decisions, rather than hoping and praying for enough early revenue to cover their sins.[38]

On rules, planning, and governance: I know lots of entrepreneurs, but I don't know any who get up in the morning looking for more or better governance or more planning or more rules. Many fly by their instincts, for better or worse, like Mondher M'henni, often successfully. Doing so can have downsides, but it has upsides, too—agility among them.

In his 2014 book *How to Turn Honey Bees into Money Bees (Without Being Stung)*, Nespresso's Éric Favre wrote, "Innovation resists planning, and those who seek it have to expect to see the spectre of failure waiting at some turns in the road."[39] Planning is essential, of course, and a key element in Pandora's ability to keep up with its runaway demand was the manufacturing planning and control system that Enevoldsen developed.

But the corporate shackles of rules, plans, and governance do not always lend themselves well to new product and new venture settings. Moving Nespresso's team outside Nestlé's headquarters unquestionably helped Gaillard and Favre get on with it and eventually break from Nestlé's conventional marketing practices with the Nespresso Club, which proved to be a pivotal marker in Nespresso's journey. Breaking the rules was something that Gaillard relished.

A final lesson from Visual Optical: It's probably not going to be a good idea if you elect to compete with your customers. Visual Optical competed with other opticians for retail trade, but tried to sell them lenses, frames, and sunglasses, too. It's little wonder that, at one point, the opticians started withholding payment of their invoices. Why pay a supplier who you perceive to be threatening your existence?

How to Add "Think Narrow, Not Broad" to *Your* Entrepreneurial Mindset

At its heart, thinking narrowly is a market segmentation challenge, as marketers call it. Every market, whatever its size, can be broken into what marketers call market segments. A market segment is a subset of the market in which the customers— or prospective customers—are similar, or behave similarly, in some way, but differently from the customers in other market segments. Ideally, what you're looking for is a segment whose customers are likely to respond to a particular product or service offering and its marketing program in a similar way. By tailoring your offering specifically for that segment—rather than offering a one-size-fits-all solution to the entire market—you should be able to better meet that segment's unique and perhaps unmet needs.[40]

So how does one segment a market, you might ask. There are three common ways to do so:

1. Segment the market demographically.
2. Segment the market geographically.
3. Segment the market by how they behave in some way: behaviorally.

Who they are—demographic segmentation: You might be tempted to segment your market by age, gender, income, education, race, or ethnic origin, or a host of other variables that essentially describe *who* people are. In B2B settings you might similarly use industry, firm size, firm age, number of employees, and so on. Arguably, this was Nespresso's approach in targeting high-income people "who have a doorman." But I suggest that, most often, you not use this all-too-common approach. Why? Two reasons:

1. Most segments defined this way (e.g., Hispanic women aged 25–44) are going to be larger and more heterogeneous than the "think narrow, not broad" mindset requires.
2. Some portions of those large segments are likely already being served, though perhaps not well for everyone within them. It's the underserved subsegment you're after.

For high-income people who were growing accustomed to barista-quality espresso at Starbucks and elsewhere, there simply was no espresso easily available for home consumption. Gaillard noticed and pounced.

Where they are—geographic segmentation: Another common approach is choosing your target market by *where* they are, geographically. Bricks-and-mortar retailers do this all the time, putting a store in a location that is accessible to those being targeted. If you want to open a shop selling fly fishing gear, you might want to locate it near a prime trout stream.

Given the global reach of the Internet today, however, geographic segmentation is on the wane, as marketers and entrepreneurs can easily reach markets anywhere, any time. My grandson in the United States received a toy last Christmas that was bought from a Chinese vendor whose web store was on Etsy's US site. Unless your opportunity involves or is targeted at specific geographic locations, you probably won't find a geographic approach particularly helpful in identifying a narrowly defined segment to target.

How they behave: behavioral segmentation: If you're looking for a more useful way to think about your target market narrowly, not broadly, behavioral segmentation is probably your answer. The essence of behavioral segmentation is that you are defining your target market based on something that the customers therein *do*. The United Kingdom's Ella's Kitchen developed colorfully packaged and tasty purees of organic fruits and vegetables for parents having trouble getting their young children to eat vegetables—a red one, a green one, a purple one, and a yellow one. Nike targeted elite distance runners, those who can run nearly a four-minute mile. Narrow, for sure. A running shoe that better met their needs soon followed. Gatorade targeted athletes who sweat profusely, thereby creating an entirely new product category we now know as sports beverages.

How might _you_ identify a behaviorally targeted market segment to serve? The key skill you'll want to build is one of achieving deep consumer insight. For Nike's Phil Knight and Bill Bowerman, that insight arose out of their _being_ the target market. Your deep insight might be similarly derived. Or, as you think narrowly, you might uncover a potential consumer problem in a target market you don't know well. In that case, there's a variety of qualitative marketing research techniques you can apply—from ethnographic observation to long interviews and more.[41] By doing so, you'll develop some new understanding of what some consumers are looking for that is not currently available. That kind of consumer understanding—coupled with the ability to develop product solutions that meet the newly discovered needs—is what led to Ella's Kitchen's, Nike's, and Gatorade's early and long-lasting success.

As you begin to identify a narrowly defined target market you wish to serve, there's one more step you'll need to take. You'll need to specify the criteria that define exactly who is in your narrowly defined segment and who is not. For Ella's kitchen, the target was British parents of toddlers who didn't like eating vegetables. For Nike, four-minute milers were in; sprinters were out. For Gatorade, the initial target were American football players in Florida, where hot and humid weather prevailed. Neither geography nor demography were central in discovering the unmet or underserved needs. But both—demography for Ella's Kitchen and geography for Nike and Gatorade—were helpful in narrowing the focus of the marketing effort that followed, thereby conserving resources.

The essence of achieving *your* **"think narrow" mindset:** Whether you're leading an effort to make an existing business more focused or you're just getting your own entrepreneurial journey underway, what we've seen here is that what you'll want to do, at least at the outset of most things new, is seek out very small market segments whose needs are not well met. The "bug list" you might have begun to develop after having read Chapter 2 may identify some customer problems that you can solve. Now that you've read Chapter 4, you can also ask, "Exactly who has those problems?" defining your answer in behavioral terms.

Closing Thoughts

There you go, a series of powerful lessons, some of which revolve around thinking narrowly, not broadly—whether for your target market or your product line—together with some steps you can take now to further develop *your* entrepreneurial mindset. While thinking narrowly is not going to guarantee the success of whatever opportunity you next pursue, it's going to enhance the depth of your understanding of what your customer wants and will pay for. It will give you a fighting chance of building a successful first platform, even if it's a small one. You can then grow from there. Among the break-the-rules mindsets that skilled entrepreneurs adopt, this mindset might be the most important of all.

5

How Entrepreneurs Get Things Done with Almost No Money: Ask for the Cash, Ride the Float

These days, many large, listed companies have so much cash on hand that they don't really know what to do with it. In many cases, the best use of it seems to be to buy back shares of their own stock from their shareholders, thereby reducing the number of shares outstanding and thereby magically increasing their company's earnings per share and, it is hoped, the share price, not to mention their own senior executives' fortunes.[1] Indeed, in 2018, Merck, the large pharmaceutical maker, spent $10 billion on research and development but a whopping $14 billion on share buy-backs and dividends.[2]

When a company is not strapped for cash, as many large companies are not, it is perhaps not surprising that managers making the everyday decisions in the trenches don't have to worry much about cash. Managing cash as if it's the last euro, dollar, pound, or rupee they've got simply isn't on their agendas. Further, those who are on bonus plans in large companies are typically incentivized on sales revenue, profits, or profit margins or earnings per share, not on cash on the balance sheet.

Accompanying this conventional thinking is an implicit assumption that doing something new requires new investment.

Accompanying this conventional thinking is an implicit assumption that doing something new requires new investment—in physical assets, in people, and more. Here's how it typically works. You figure out how much investment you need to get the project started. You forecast the cash flows that the project will deliver in the future—its revenues net of its expenses. If you went to business school, you then use what you learned in your finance courses to calculate the project's return on investment (ROI), net present value, or whatever your company deems the appropriate metric.

If the ROI is good enough—passing the so-called "hurdle rate"—and better than any alternative uses to which those funds can be put (and if it works its way around any political barriers!), the project is approved, and the cash is provided from the company treasury. All very neat and tidy and theoretically sound. But what about cash-starved entrepreneurs?

Some entrepreneurs think differently: For most entrepreneurs, cash is the lifeblood that enables their company's survival against the long odds. Run out of it, and you're in deep trouble. But cash, to entrepreneurs, at least in the early stages of any new venture, is very expensive. Why? Today's conventional wisdom suggests that to get your hands on the cash you require, you should knock on the door of an investor. If the investor likes you, and likes what you are doing, she'll give you some cash. And she'll want a stake in your business, on terms that you probably won't like very much. Venture capital, they call it.

Many of today's entrepreneurs have drunk this venture capital Kool-Aid, perhaps for good reason, given the plethora of great companies and wealthy founders that this system has produced. Come up with a great idea. Write a killer business plan. Raise some venture capital. And, "*Voilà!*" you'll be rich. Or so the thinking goes.[3] But the fruits of *your* endeavors in building the business will then flow in part—and perhaps in their entirety—to those who ponied up the money. Control, too. That may not be what you had in mind when you considered becoming an entrepreneur!

But what if you could break this "investment comes first" rule? What if you didn't need to go hat-in-hand to an investor to get the cash you need to start or grow your business? Or, if you're toiling away in the trenches of a large company, what if you didn't have to go to the "capital committee" and ask for the cash your new project requires? What if you could simply ask your customers for the cash you need—in the form of revenue for what you're about to sell them—and use that cash to start and grow your business? These powerful, counter-conventional, and potentially life-changing questions are what this chapter is about.

What you're in for in Chapter 5: First, let's be clear what I mean by "ask for the cash" and "ride the float." I mean the following: After (courageously) asking for and getting payment from your customers as early as possible (ideally before you make or deliver what they've agreed to buy) and after convincing your key suppliers to take payment from you as late as possible (perhaps 30 or 60 or 90 days after they've shipped you what you ordered), you'll find your bank account flush with cash, at least until you have to pay your suppliers.

While you have that cash in hand—the "float" before you have to pay it to your suppliers—you can use it to grow your business. Buy inventory. Hire people. Buy more Google AdWords. And so on. As your business grows, you then use your future revenue to pay your suppliers and your people, just in time when their bills come due. That's exactly what 19-year-old Michael Dell did in 1984 to start Dell Computer. And it's mostly how he grew Dell, too.[4] So how will this chapter bring this simple and potentially life-changing principle to life so *you* can apply it?

We'll first examine a little-discussed fact about Tesla, and the lesson that Elon Musk's insights about cash have held for its astonishing growth and potentially even more astonishing potential. We'll unpack the story of one of the early online travel agents, Budgetplaces.com, that built its business and achieved a lucrative exit for its founder entirely by asking its traveler customers for cash up front and riding the float.

On the downside, we'll also examine an ill-fated series of decisions that led to the devastating and sudden downfall of The Loot, a once fast-growing retailer of casual apparel in India. We'll then close the chapter with some powerful lessons learned and some steps you can take now to make "Ask for the cash, ride the float" a part of *your* entrepreneurial mindset. Buckle up and enjoy the ride!

Tesla: A Customer-Funded Carmaker? Really?

"The company that Elon Musk built to usher in the electric-car future might not have enough cash to make it through the calendar year." So wrote Bloomberg analysts Dana Hull and Hannah Recht on April 30, 2018.[5] Indeed, though not quite that soon, in May 2019 Musk raised $2.7 billion, a mixture of $860 million in equity and $1.84 billion in debt.[6] But Musk, noted for his prowess at raising money from investors and lenders, has another gift for which he's much less appreciated. He asks his customers to pay deposits in advance in order to get their hands on the wheel of one of his hot-selling cars when it rolls off the assembly line.

It's Musk's view that if you've built something that customers simply have to have, they will queue up to get it and pay deposits in advance to secure their place in the queue. That cash, paid well in advance at multiple points in Tesla's journey, was used to hire automotive engineers, to build new factories, and to do what was necessary to keep Tesla on the road to survival and more.

> **If you've built something that customers simply have to have, they will queue up to get it and pay deposits in advance.**

Musk first put this gift to use at a series of events in 2006 at which Tesla's plans to build the Roadster, its initial model, were unveiled. Dozens of attendees at the Pebble Beach Concourse d'Elegance wrote $100,000 checks on the spot to pre-order their cars. "This was long before Kickstarter," recalls Marc Tarpenning, a Tesla co-founder. "But then we started getting millions of dollars at these types of events."[7] Within three weeks Tesla sold out of its initial offering of 100 Roadsters. A cool $10 million was in the bank with which to build the cars.[8]

Cars Roll Out; More Funding Rolls In

Tesla's plan was straightforward. "Build a sports car. Use that money to build an affordable car. Use that money to build an even more affordable car. While doing this, also provide zero-emission electric power generation options."[9] That's what Tesla's founders Martin Eberhard and Marc Tarpenning, battery entrepreneur Jeffrey Straubel, and Musk agreed to in 2006, not long after Musk had joined the founding team, by bringing to the party his own $6.3 million investment, which constituted 90 percent of that investment round!

The Roadster debuted in 2008, a year later than expected, sporting cutting-edge battery technology and an all-electric powertrain, for a hefty price tag north of $100,000. Early Roadsters could travel 250 miles on a single charge but charging them was slow and unit sales were modest. With the company burning cash fast, and with the onset of the global financial crisis roiling financial markets everywhere, on Christmas Eve 2008 Musk managed to secure a debt deal of $40 million, this time contributing a further $20 million of his own money, matched by his early investors.[10] Tesla had secured the lifeline it needed to stay in business. But Tesla needed more cash.

In May 2009, Daimler AG, the German maker of the Mercedes Benz, joined the party with a $50 million investment for a 10 percent stake, as part of a deal in which Tesla would provide battery packs for a new electric version of Daimler's Smart car. The deal was sealed when Tesla engineers refitted a used Mexican-built Smart car, which "converted with the instant torque of an electric motor, suddenly became a hellcat."[11]

Tesla's Diarmid O'Connell recalls the jubilation over the Daimler deal. "Here is the company that invented the internal combustion engine, and they are investing in us. It's not just our scientists saying this stuff is good. It's Mercedes freaking Benz!"[12] In January 2010, the US Department of Energy, which was at the time frantically bailing out the American automobile industry to preserve its jobs, came on board, too, with a $465 million loan.[13]

"Tesla had, in effect, bought a 5.3 million square foot factory for next to nothing!"

Then fortune struck. With the global auto industry struggling with excess capacity due to the great recession, Toyota sold its Fremont, California, plant, which it had planned to shut down, to Tesla in May 2010 for a paltry $42 million, agreeing also to invest $50 million in Tesla for a 2.5 percent stake. Tesla had, in effect, acquired a 5.3 million square foot factory for next to nothing![14] Less than a month later, Tesla went public on NASDAQ, raising another $226 million, followed by another public offering a year later that raised another $158 million. The stage was set for what was to follow.

Financing Tesla's Future

To this point in its journey, Tesla had relied primarily on round after round of investment, much of which had come from Musk himself, thanks to the money he'd made as an early investor and executive at PayPal. But he'd also required customers to put down substantial deposits to reserve a Roadster or a Tesla Model S, the next car in the plan. Though those deposits surely helped keep Tesla alive, the very modest unit sales of Tesla's very pricey cars meant that they didn't nearly add up to what Tesla required. That was about to change, but it took Musk a few years—and too many nights sleeping on the factory floor!—to work out the kinks.

By early 2013, with the Fremont factory finally beginning to ramp up production, Tesla was beginning to both see and deliver good news. The venerable *Motor Trend* magazine selected the new Model S as its 2013 Car of the Year and put Musk on its cover. Musk organized an all-hands-on-deck sales drive, with the goal of selling—and delivering—4,750 cars in Q1, a figure that CFO Deepak Ahuja had assured Musk would make Tesla profitable for the quarter. On the last Saturday of March 2013, car number 4,750 was delivered. Sales for the quarter totaled $329 million, some 80 percent of the entire previous year's revenue![15]

Tesla's stock price took off, tripling in Q2, enabling Musk to raise another $1.7 billion in new shares and debt, using part of the proceeds to pay off the US government loan. More subtly, however, and not widely noticed, deposits of $5,000 for the basic model of its latest car, the snazzy Model X crossover SUV with its gull-winged rear doors, and $40,000 for the Signature model, quickly rolled in. By June 2015, an estimated 24,000 customers had placed deposits bringing in well north of $100 million.[16] Musk was asking for cash from his customers, not just the stock market, and they were responding!

Musk Paints Another "Ask for the Cash" Picture

In March 2016, Tesla introduced its most affordable car yet, the Model 3. On day one, 200,000 deposits were taken at $1,000 each, generating $200 million in new cash, a number that soon grew to a cool half billion. But Musk was not done finding ways to ask for cash. In August 2016, with confidence having been built in Tesla at last, he asked his key suppliers to change their terms. He also asked key suppliers for retroactive discounts on what Tesla had already paid them. Tesla would now pay their invoices in 60 days, up from the typical 30 days, he announced. Speaking to industry analysts, he described the move as "the nirvana" that would allow Tesla to "make the car and get paid for it before the bill is due to suppliers. Obviously, that's like the promised land right there," he crowed.[17]

> **With customers flocking to the Tesla website in droves to put their money down, and with Tesla now paying its suppliers long after its cars had been built, Tesla had become a customer-funded and supplier-enabled cash machine.**

With customers flocking to the Tesla website in droves to put their money down, and with Tesla now paying its suppliers long after its cars had been built, Tesla had become a customer-funded and supplier-enabled cash machine. By Q2 2018, Tesla's deposits across its three models—the Models S, X, and 3—totaled $985 million.[18]

In July 2018, Musk went a step further, making a change to the deposit structure for customers. Deposits had always been refundable; customers weren't committed to following through with the purchase, and Tesla couldn't be guaranteed a sale. From this point forward, Musk required an additional $2,500 deposit to "fulfill" the order.[19] The deposits for the Model 3 would include a $100 nonrefundable order fee along with a refundable $2,500 deposit, and this would become the same for the Model Y in March 2019. The change was said to deter some speculative buyers and give Tesla a more accurate projection of future sales. But what did it really do? It gave Tesla even more of its customers' cash!

Revenue Is Vanity; Profit Is Sanity; Cash Is Reality

For years, we've read, off and on, about Tesla's struggles with its revenues not meeting targets and with profit falling short of analysts' expectations. Nevertheless, as I write in 2022, Tesla has become one of the world's most highly valued companies, having topped the $1 trillion valuation mark, at least for a while, before a stock market sell-off knocked billions off its and other companies' gaudy market caps. Will its valuation continue to soar? Will it continue to flourish, despite its long odds? Perhaps we should not count Elon Musk out.

Surprisingly, at least to most observers, Tesla has not needed to raise any further equity since May 2019. Who needs investors—or bankers, either—when your customers are so excited about what you offer that they are willing to fund your business, with what amount to interest-free loans, at that! As Bruce Sidlinger, already an owner of two Tesla vehicles reported, "The morning after the Roadster was announced, I put a deposit down . . . Elon Musk is one of our planet's great hopes. I would offer a kidney to him if he needed it."[20] Thus, here's a question for you: Can *you* find a way to get *your* customers to fund *your* business as generously as Musk has at Tesla? Perhaps, with the right mindset and a compelling offer, you can!

Budgetplaces.com: Thank You, Google![21]

Fortunately for John Erceg, his girlfriend (and now wife) Lucia was a dentist, making good money. With the allure of entrepreneurship in the air in Barcelona, and with four years under his belt as a product manager for Hewlett-Packard, Erceg decided to take the entrepreneurial plunge. So far, however, his progress had fallen far short of his dreams. He'd lost €50,000 and two years of his life on his first start-up, selling software that promised a new paradigm in digital printing. His second venture, printing digital photos for tourists in Barcelona, only cost him another €7,000. "At least I was failing quicker and cheaper," he recalls. "And FotoMoto was a ridiculous idea when I look back at it. It deserved to fail."[22]

It was 2003 and Erceg still wanted to be an entrepreneur. "I just want a simple business that I can explain easily," he decided. "No more new paradigms or endless PowerPoint presentations."[23] The couple pooled their savings, secured a mortgage, and bought a small flat near the Barcelona Cathedral to rent out to tourists. Erceg spruced up the flat and began posting flyers around town, renting the flat a few days at a time. A year later, with rentals more than paying the mortgage, he and Lucia bought another flat. They soon realized that they needed to build a website, as they now offered a greater supply of room-nights than they could fill locally.

With the new website up and running, Erceg started knocking on doors, signing up family-run budget hotels, most of which lacked any presence on the Internet. He soon found himself not only booking and managing his and Lucia's two flats, but also running a small travel website that represented a growing number of properties around Barcelona. Most of his clients were young travelers from northern European countries, looking for somewhere cheap to stay, to match the cheap flights they had booked on one of the new budget airlines that were growing fast.

Becoming an Internet Entrepreneur

Erceg decided to build a new and more elaborate website that listed hotels, hostels, and apartments, as long as they were budget options, at around €60 for a double room. The deal for both travelers and the hotels was simple. Erceg would collect from the traveler 15 percent of the total booking at the time the booking was made. The traveler would pay the balance directly to the hotel upon check-in.

With a typical stay of five nights, Erceg was collecting an average of €45 from his travelers' credit cards. He discovered that he could reliably generate bookings by spending around 55 percent of his revenue, around €25, on the newfangled AdWords which Google had recently introduced. As there was no further

> **He discovered that he could reliably generate bookings by spending around 55 percent of his revenue, around €25, on the newfangled AdWords which Google had recently introduced.**

paperwork to do with the hotels, Erceg could put the remaining €20 to work to grow his business—hiring someone to sign up more hotels and cover his other costs.

By 2005 he built the Barcelona inventory to 90 properties. Emboldened by this success, Erceg convinced Lucia's brother to move to Madrid and start recruiting budget hotels there. "People often say 'Don't mix friends and family with business,' and there is certainly some wisdom in that statement, but I knew he was a good guy and that I could trust him. I felt that a 'known unknown' was much better than hiring, in a remote office, an 'unknown unknown,'" Erceg recalled.[24]

With the Madrid market developing nicely, Erceg hired a translator, added Paris, and launched his three websites—Barcelona, Madrid, and Paris—in French and Spanish, as well as in English. "The focus was now 100% on getting the cheap accommodations—and *all* of them in Barcelona and Madrid!—and we realised the key was to have feet on the ground in each new market we entered. A face-to-face relationship with the properties, plus a simple one-page contract, mattered!"[25] By the autumn of 2006, Erceg's business was showing the potential to become something more substantial than had been apparent at the outset.

Discovering Float

Erceg's approach to this point had been to manage his business on a daily basis with a simple Excel sheet that tracked the cash coming in from new bookings and the cash going out for AdWords and his other expenses. In addition to the 55 percent of his revenue he was spending to get bookings, he spent another 45 percent on the rest—people, IT, a bit of rent, and so on. The result was a break-even business. No profit each month, and no loss. "But what about cash?" you might wonder.

❝Erceg was getting 45 days' float from the bookings made just before the end of each month, and 75 days' float for bookings made at the beginning of the month.❞

Fortunately, Google's payment terms allowed Erceg to pay for each month's AdWords on the 15th of the following month. Even better, Google was willing to take payment from a credit card, which gave Erceg another month before the AdWords were paid for. Erceg was getting 45 days' float from the bookings made just before the end of each month, and 75 days' float for bookings made at the beginning of the month.

What this meant for Erceg was that, on October 15, 2006, for example, he owed Google for the AdWords he'd bought in August. But 55 percent of August's revenue was a smaller figure than 55 percent of October's revenue, as the business was growing. That meant there was cash left over in October and most every month, typically around 10 percent of sales after paying the rest of his bills!

What did Erceg do with this extra cash? He used every euro of spare cash to buy more AdWords! It was a virtuous cycle. His travelers paid for their bookings the day they made them, and Erceg's key supplier, Google (whose AdWords represented the main cost of getting each booking), was paid an average of 60 days later! Riding the float was growing Erceg's business inexorably, and in measurable and predictable fashion.

Ramping Up

With the growth in bookings that Madrid and Paris were delivering, Erceg decided to expand his coverage of European cities and add German and Italian versions of all of his sites. He sent trusted staffers to sign up budget properties in another seven cities. By September 2007, gross bookings and revenues nearly tripled over January's level, with the business generating €75,000 in profit, up from €12,000 in January.

With a growing and now solidly profitable business, Erceg saw the pattern he had unknowingly created. "In the company we had a lot of young, multi-lingual people who loved Barcelona, but they didn't always stay for very long. If someone wanted to move to Rome, I decided okay, let's set up a hotel recruiter in Rome! This was opportunistic, vs. top-down, strategic planning. I believe much more in betting on a known person, than to go blindly to some city for strategic reasons and hire someone who I have no connection with."[26]

Until 2008, each of Erceg's destinations was represented by a separate website, each with a different domain name. As this arrangement was proving difficult to manage in what had become an SEO/SEM world, the time was right to build an umbrella brand. Budgetplaces.com was born.

By the end of the year, Erceg was sitting pretty, despite having had to dip into his savings to get through a brief downturn in travel caused by the global financial crisis earlier that year. Gross bookings, all funded by the float that Erceg was riding so skillfully, nearly doubled over the prior year, from €17 million in 2007 to €30 million in 2008. And 15 percent of every booking was his, paid by his travelers an average of 60 days before his Google invoice came due!

> **Gross bookings, all funded by the float that Erceg was riding so skillfully, nearly doubled over the prior year, from €17 million in 2007 to €30 million in 2008.**

The 2009 Land Grab

One of the members of Erceg's advisory board pointed out that, since the company had escaped the financial crisis largely unscathed and was performing well, it was a good time to ramp up the business. This would mean rapidly expanding both the number of destinations and the number of properties available. "Spending money to acquire properties without enough demand for bookings," Erceg cautioned, "is a recipe for losing money, as is the opposite, spending money to get bookings without enough rooms to accommodate them. It's an extremely delicate balance—unless you've got money to waste, that is, like some of our better-funded competitors, which we haven't."[27]

Erceg was still walking a delicate financial tightrope, spending every spare euro to grow his business. There was little margin for error. But he decided on an audacious move. He would ramp up the acquisition of more properties and more new destinations. Simultaneously, he would ramp up his company's SEO and SEM capabilities. It was essential, he knew, for growth in bookings to keep pace with the growth in available properties.

Erceg's efforts paid off, generating 1,000 new properties in now more than 50 cities, plus an increase in gross bookings to nearly €40 million in 2009. His company was still taking 15 percent of each booking from most of its properties, so Erceg found himself with a business earning nearly €1 million in pre-tax profits on the €6 million in revenue that represented his company's share of the €40 million in gross bookings it had made. The business, which he and Lucia (who was by now his wife and the mother of his young children) owned in its entirety, had come a long way.

Time to Sell?

In late 2009, Erceg received an unsolicited call from the CEO of a European competitor in the online travel agency (OTA) industry.

"Would he sell?" Erceg was asked. After a considerable amount of back-and-forth, Erceg concluded that there might be other prospective suitors around. An abundance of capital was flowing into the OTA industry, he observed, and consolidation was beginning to occur. Well-funded, fast-growing VC-backed online travel agents—Expedia, Booking.com, and others—were jockeying for position.

After a lengthy, stressful, and exhausting process, with bidders coming to the table and some backing away as their own circumstances changed, in 2010 Erceg sold a majority stake in his business to a private equity player, netting a substantial, life-changing eight-figure sum. Not a bad payday for seven years' work in a business that had taken virtually no investment—ever. It had been funded by its 15 percent share of its travelers' bookings—their cash in advance—and by riding the 60 days of float provided by Google's payment terms. As Erceg admits, "Google created my business. I exist because of Google. I was very lucky."[28] Thank you, Google!

The Loot: "I'd Always Had Profits. . ."[29]

By the time Jay Gupta enrolled at college in Mumbai in 1994, it was already clear that an entrepreneurial path was for him. In Mumbai he observed the enthusiasm with which young style-conscious Indians were snapping up the latest Western fashion brands. "I've always believed on-the-job learning was much more educational than something like an MBA," he recalled, explaining his next move.[30] He convinced a few apparel vendors to give him some merchandise on consignment,* leased a tiny 200-square-foot retail space near his home in Vashi, a Mumbai

---

*"Goods on consignment" meant that the ownership of the goods remained with the original vendor until the goods were sold by the consignee, at which point the consignee paid the original vendor for the goods. Unsold goods could be returned to the vendor by the consignee.

suburb, and held a series of temporary exhibitions at which he sold T-shirts and denim jeans, along with more traditional Indian outfits. His learning about apparel retailing—licenses, permits, what sells and what doesn't, and much more—had begun.

A year later, thanks to financing from his family, Gupta purchased the retail space and opened a full-fledged store called Casual Plus. It featured top Western brands such as Reebok footwear and Lee jeans. It thrived. He then leveraged the success of Casual Plus into deals to open four single-brand stores for Western brands and one for an Indian brand. Still learning, Gupta had an insight that would shape his retailing philosophy going forward. "I saw that 98 percent of customers in these Western sportswear and casual apparel stores wanted discounts."[31]

> **Nearly all of his merchandise was bought on consignment, which meant he did not have to pay for the goods until after they were sold.**

A franchised factory outlet store for Adidas followed in 1999, selling seconds and closeouts at bargain prices. Five more factory outlets came next, for Western brands Levi and Nike and Indian brands Provogue, ColourPlus, and Weekender. Nearly all of his merchandise was bought on consignment, which meant he did not have to pay for the goods after they were sold. He was living in working capital Nirvana!

By 2004, Gupta was operating 10 different stores under three different formats—multibrand, full-price franchised single-brand, and factory outlets—also single-brand. Could he create a fourth format, he wondered, that would combine for consumers the best attributes of all three?

The Loot Is Born

In June 2004, Gupta opened The Loot, choosing the name because it connoted "steal" in both Hindi and English. He signed up a famous Bollywood villain, Gulshan Grover, as his brand ambassador. Grover's image peered ominously from behind the cash counter, setting forth what the store stood for: "No fakes. No seconds. Guaranteed price. Guaranteed product. And 25% to 60% off, 365 days per year."[32] Fitting rooms were dressed up as prison cells.

Not all of Gupta's suppliers were happy with the new format, however, fearing it would undercut their full-priced offerings elsewhere. Gupta didn't want to take their seconds, either. But some brands faced with serious overstocks and substandard factory outlets came on board. "You'll sell our products in a dignified manner," one of them remarked.[33]

The new format took off, generating considerably more revenue during the store's first two months than had any of his previous openings. "I knew I was on to something really big," Gupta exclaimed. He quickly sought and won permission from all but two of his franchisors to let him turn eight of his existing stores into The Loot concept. "Suddenly, we had real impact on the Mumbai retailing scene. More important, with nine stores operating under the same format, we now had the buying power that we sorely needed."[34]

Reality Strikes

Along with the changes in his retail format, Gupta also wanted more control over the merchandise he bought and sold. So he decided that, instead of accepting whatever styles his vendors wanted to give him under the previous consignment arrangements, he would pay for the goods outright, as and when closeout opportunities presented themselves. Suddenly, his bedroom no longer sufficed as a warehouse. Overhead skyrocketed, as his team grew and as fees and local taxes that his franchisors had previously paid fell onto his shoulders now.

By the end March 2005, despite a now-larger credit line from his bank, his company was seriously stretched for cash. Inventory ballooned, and not all of it was saleable. But it wasn't written off, either, a step that might have scared the bank, on which Gupta was highly dependent. Another lesson had landed with a thud.

> I'd always had profits and I always had the cash I need-ed to operate. I had failed to appreciate the difference between profits and cash flow. It shook me up to see the cash disappear when I started flipping the stores and add-ing corporate overheads.

And a burgeoning load of inventory, too. "Am I going to make it?" he worried.[35]

Experience to the Rescue

R. P. Chhabra, a recently retired banker and father of one of Gupta's good friends, began joining the duo as they met from time to time to discuss The Loot's struggles, which were mount-ing, due in part to the increased credit lines that Gupta had maxed out and the heavy interest burden they bore. In early 2006, Chhabra signed on formally as a part-time consultant, and by autumn 2006 Gupta anointed him CEO. They quickly raised some outside capital, built an experienced team, centralized buy-ing, and put structured systems and procedures in place. The cash situation began to improve.

But scaling the business was, so far, elusive, as dealing with local complexities to open new stores in outlying cities and towns was proving difficult. Worse, the business was still walking a financial tightrope. Then, in November 2006, S. K. Desai, a busi-nessman in Surat who was operating franchised stores for several other retail brands, approached Gupta. Desai wanted to know whether Gupta would offer him a franchise in Surat.

Gupta and Chhabra quickly realized that changing the model yet again would have powerful implications for the company's cash flow. Not only would The Loot be paid a franchise fee up front, when a new franchisee was signed, but the inventory in the store would be held by— and financed by—the franchisee! Gupta figured that, in the first year alone, a new franchised store would generate some 3.8 million rupees in cash to The Loot, compared to 800,000 rupees for a company-owned store, a difference of 3 million rupees (around $60,000 US). In subsequent years, The Loot would get a 10 percent royalty on the franchisee's sales (expected to be around 240,000 rupees or $5,000), with far fewer headaches to manage.

> **Not only would The Loot be paid a franchise fee up front, when a new franchisee was signed, but the inventory in the store would be held by—and financed by—the franchisee!**

Growth Takes Off, But Not for Long

By mid-2011, the store count skyrocketed to 155, with 110 franchises in 70 cities across India, owned by nearly 50 franchisees. There were an additional 45 company-owned stores in Mumbai, Delhi, and Pune. This growth was largely funded by cash flow— mainly the franchisees' cash in advance for the franchise fees— plus credit lines from banks.

Along the way, however, the Indian government, in search of tax revenue, had imposed a series of taxes on businesses, among them a 12.5 percent services tax that hit 80 percent of The Loot's cost structure, as well as those of most other retailers in India. The retailing industry protested and won a stay. It was widely expected that the tax would be repealed. Alas, it was not, and in 2011 the verdict landed. The Loot owed 12.5 percent back taxes on 80 percent of its cost structure, an untenable sum that totaled 5 percent of its last three years' sales!

In order to ensure collection of the services tax, the regulations specified that retail landlords were required to collect the taxes from their lessees. Gupta, having not anticipated the unfavorable ruling, had not set aside any funds, and simply had no cash to pay what its 40-odd landlords were required to collect. The result? Landlords put locks on the company-owned stores, in order to get their hands on the inventory and fixtures therein. What about the 110 franchised stores, you wonder? They, too, were hit hard by the back taxes due, and most had no cash to pay The Loot for the previous month's shipments. They stopped paying and stopped ordering, too, as the new taxes rendered their low-margin businesses unviable.

Needless to say, things got very messy, and The Loot's high-wire act was over. By 2013, all but five company-owned stores had closed, and the rest were gone by December 2015. Looking back, The Loot's best days were during two periods of time: those when it was procuring its merchandise on consignment, enabling it to ride its vendors' float and pay for the goods after they were sold; and those prior to the tax verdict, when it turned to a franchise model, getting cash in advance from franchise fees. Without one source of up-front cash or the other, The Loot's business model, with its very modest gross margins, simply was not viable.

Lessons Learned About Asking for Cash and Riding the Float—and More

As you've seen in this chapter, there are two fundamental elements involved in "asking for the cash and riding the float," which can be pursued independently or (even better) simultaneously:

1. Ask your customer to pay at the time of purchase (as Budgetplaces.com and The Loot did) or even sooner (Tesla's deposits, paid months or years in advance).

2. Ask one or more key suppliers to let you pay them as late as you can (Tesla's push for 60-day terms, once it had established credibility as a going concern; Budgetplaces.com and Google's "next month" terms; Loot's buying on consignment from its vendors).

Putting these two sides of the coin together reveals that what counts is the number of days of separation between the day the customer's cash comes in and the day the supplier's cash goes out, along with the magnitude of the float involved. For Elon Musk, the number of days of cash in advance was exceptionally large—months, even years, until a new model began shipping and production capacity caught up with the number of orders that had been placed. And the magnitude was substantial too, amounting to nearly 100 percent of the purchase price for his first Tesla Roadsters. For John Erceg, the 60 days of float were effectively coming from his key supplier, Google, whose AdWords cost nearly half the revenue from each booking.

On the audacity it can take: Elon Musk's audacity to ask for $100,000 deposits for a Tesla Roadster that existed only in his and has partners' minds is legendary. "We just had not thought of trying to do that," recalled Marc Tarpenning, years later. And once Musk saw his customers get out their checkbooks, it became a pattern that Tesla would follow with every launch. John Erceg, as well, had the audacity in 2009 to pursue a land-grab to list hotels and B&Bs all over Europe, despite the financial tightrope on which his company, thanks to Google's generous terms, was walking. As the saying goes, "If you don't ask, you don't get."

If you're a leader trying to get your people to think and act more counter-conventionally—and even to break some "here's how we've always done things around here" rules—then getting them to ask for the customers' cash to fund their new projects might be a great jumping-off point for such a journey.

❝The pace of growth, and how that growth gets funded, is a choice every entrepreneur, whether on her own journey or employed elsewhere, can make. ❞

On full versus partial funding: As we've seen from Budgetplaces .com, sometimes asking for the cash and riding the float can fund essentially all of what a growing business requires. But had Erceg wished to grow even faster, he'd have needed more money. The pace of growth, and how that growth gets funded, is a choice every entrepreneur, whether on her own journey or employed elsewhere, can make. For Loot, getting goods on consignment was only part of the funding story, too. Willing bankers stepped in, time after time. For Tesla, even the billions that Musk raised in customer deposits were insufficient to fully fund the operations of a new automobile maker in that capital-intensive industry. But without his customers' deposits, Tesla might well not have survived.

Thus, the customer's money, received up front, and your suppliers' money paid slowly, thanks to generous terms, don't have to fully fund your business. But they can make the difference between survival and death—and can mean owning your business outright, with the freedom and control that doing so entails!

On the power of prototypes: Having the ability to "wow" your customer, or some other provider of cash, with a stunning prototype is sometimes the key that will unlock their funds. A hacked Smart car unlocked a $50 million cash infusion from Daimler at a crucial point in Tesla's journey. For Jay Gupta, his successful apparel exhibitions were instrumental in convincing suppliers to deal with him on a consignment basis when he opened CasualPlus. *Demonstrating* to suppliers and others that you will perform for them delivers a much stronger message than simply *saying* you'll perform.

I often hear entrepreneurs say they require seed funding to build their initial prototype. I always respond, "Not so!" In my first entrepreneurial venture, I convinced a high school metal shop teacher to have his students undertake, as a class project, building the prototype I needed, for free. It was win-win for the students and for me.

On "complete" entrepreneurial teams: Often, what it takes to get the first version of your product built—whether it's software or something more physical in nature—is what I call a "complete" entrepreneurial team. You probably want to have someone on your founding team that can actually build the first prototype (and maybe more of them, as the first one will probably not be quite right!), rather than finding investment to pay someone else to build it.

Too often, I find, aspiring entrepreneurs come up with a promising problem to solve and an idea for a potentially compelling solution. Too quickly, they then start spending precious time seeking capital with which to get a prototype built. A better course of action, in my experience, is to add a complementary member to the founding team, one who can build a "minimum viable product" with little or no investment.

That's what Airbnb co-founders Brian Chesky and Joe Gebbia did in adding programmer Nathan Blecharczyk to their team early-on.[36] As best-selling author Steve Blank reminds us, a minimum viable product (MVP) is all you need to get your journey underway.[37] That MVP will help your customer make peace with handing over some cash up front, as Tesla's hacking a Smart car did for Daimler.

On the learning journey required: Elon Musk did not know whether prospective buyers would part with $100,000 up front to get their hands on an early Roadster. John Erceg didn't know up front that his traveler customers would pay 15 percent up front to "secure the booking." Erceg didn't know up front that he would have to delicately balance supply with demand: get some bookings, add more hotels, get more bookings, and so on. Jay Gupta didn't know what lessons he would learn from each of his new formats until he got them open, one after another.

At the end of the day, starting something new, whether at a kitchen table, in a co-working space, or deep inside an established business almost always initiates a learning journey. But that journey is not only about what the customers want and will pay for. It's also about how best to get them to pay as far in advance as you can.

On the power of trusted relationships: In his early days, John Erceg's approach to getting new hotels onto his site was ingenious. He pounded the pavement and knocked on doors, personally at first, then delegating that role, always to people he already knew and trusted, starting with his brother-in-law! The earnest face-to-face contact to build trust, plus a simple one-page contract, plus the opportunity for marketing-starved budget hotels to fill more room nights proved to be a compelling combination.

Similarly, Jay Gupta's careful attention to paying his first vendors on time won their trust, which enabled him to open his first single-vendor stores. Simply put, trust pays, with employees, customers, and suppliers alike.

On the difference between cash flow and profit: Jay Gupta "always had profits," in his words. But once he abandoned his consignment model, he rarely had cash flow, due to the inventory that was growing as fast as his top line grew, and sometimes faster. Generous bankers made up the difference with their ever-growing credit lines.

Tesla, in its early years as a listed company, was another story. Profits didn't come until almost three years after Tesla's IPO. The analysts would write shrill headlines, wringing their hands and crying their warnings about Tesla's dismal profit performance. And so it was.

❝Which would you rather have? Jay Gupta's profits with bankers breathing down his neck? Or Musk's customer-funded cash?❞

But cash flow? There were some tight spots, to be sure, as we've seen in this chapter. But, for the most part, Musk had learned that his fervently rapturous customers would keep their deposits flowing, new model after new model. Which would you rather have? Jay Gupta's profits with bankers breathing down his neck? Or Musk's customer-funded cash?[38] It's your call.

Bonus Lessons Learned

This chapter has delivered another set of powerful lessons, in hopes of enabling and encouraging you to ask for the cash and to ride *your* float. But there are other lessons here, too, as one might expect from the always audacious, ever provocative Elon Musk.

On the power of building your personal brand: The loyalty, even reverence, that Musk has generated across his various businesses from Tesla to Solar City to SpaceX and more is a thing to behold. As 60-year-old aerospace engineer Bruce Sidlinger confided to writers Dana Hall and Hanna Recht, after slapping down his deposit for one of Tesla's newest Roadsters, "Putting down $50,000 for a Roadster that won't be out for a few years is kind of like buying a bond that returns zero."[39]

What's remarkable about Sidlinger is that he was, at the time, already the proud owner of both a Model S and a Model X. Earlier in 2018, he had driven more than 2,000 miles from Arizona to Florida in one of his Teslas so he could watch the launch of a rocket made by another of Musk's companies, SpaceX.

On getting cash from your customers and suppliers—and who else? As we've seen, Musk's uncanny ability to generate cash from his customers and suppliers to fund his company's growth has been, and continues to be, a key ingredient in Tesla's journey. But it's not the only ingenious way Musk has found to generate cash.

Musk discovered early on that the state of California required automakers to sell a certain proportion of "green" cars. Happily for Tesla, automakers that could not hit their required targets were allowed to buy credits from other car manufacturers if the others had exceeded the state target.

Since 100 percent of Tesla's cars qualified for the credit, it had excess credits to sell.

Between 2008 and 2017 the sale of these credits to other car manufacturers accounted for $1.3 billion of additional cash.[40] Can you imagine getting paid by your competitors? Musk can—and does! Did Musk influence the adoption of such a provision in the California law? We'll probably never know.

Surprisingly, perhaps, government mandates like this one or programs of one kind or another can be very meaningful sources of cash. Pobble, an innovative UK company that provides online tools to help primary school teachers help kids learn to write—and post their writing online for others to see—has funded a substantial portion of its software development costs by obtaining government R&D grants.[41] Perhaps you can, too!

How to Add "Ask for the Cash, Ride the Float" to *Your* Entrepreneurial Mindset

The audacity of Elon Musk to ask for $100,000 to reserve a yet-to-be built Roadster, or a more modest sum for a new Model 3. The courage of John Erceg to keep spending every spare euro to buy more AdWords. The personal conviction of both that they were on sound paths. The trust that Jay Gupta built with his suppliers. The self-belief of all three that, in the end, they would do what it takes to survive and succeed, no matter the prior odds. It's your own personal attributes—*your* mindset—that make this kind of "ask for the cash" funding possible.

These attributes—audacity, courage, trustworthiness, faith in oneself—are not part of everyone's personality, to be sure. Setting forth on an entrepreneurial path, whether from your garage or within an established business, is not for everyone, either. But if the entrepreneurial path is one you wish to pursue, in one way or another, there's no better or more hospitable way to finance your jour-

❝Setting forth on an entrepreneurial path, whether from your garage or in an established business, is not for everyone. ❞

ney than by finding a need that's so compelling for your customers that they'll pay you up front, and finding suppliers that will take payment later, if only because they trust you and they believe you'll bring value to their business, too.

If you're up for adding these kinds of attributes to *your* entrepreneurial mindset, a good place to start might be to pick up a copy of Carol Dweck's wonderful book, *Mindset*.[42] You may already have the kind of "growth mindset" that Dweck so powerfully elucidates. If you do, you'll find yourself in a good place to simply begin demonstrating the audacity, courage, trustworthiness, and faith in yourself that will enable and encourage you to ask for the cash and break the "investment comes first" rule. And don't forget to ask your suppliers for favourable terms either, terms that will provide you with more days of float than you might otherwise get. You'll be glad you did!

Closing Thoughts

Whether you get the cash you need—and whether it's to get started or to grow—from customers who pay early or from suppliers you can pay late, or from other unconventional or counterconventional sources, the sheer beauty of all of this kind of finance is what it costs you—nothing! You don't have to pay it back with interest, like a bank loan. You don't have to give up a stake in your business to a possibly rapacious or unhelpful investor.

And once you've figured out a model that will work in your setting, as Tesla and Budgetplaces.com did to finance much of their journeys, it's a counter-conventional gift that keeps on giving! Do you really need investment up front to get your innovation underway or to ramp up its growth rate, if you're already well down that path? I hope I've convinced you that you can break that rule!

6

Make the Future Winnings Yours!: Beg, Borrow, But Don't Steal

Among the most well developed of the practices that help large companies try to innovate is the way in which new initiatives are proposed, approved, and funded. As you saw in Chapter 4, there's typically a series of stages and gates though which proposed new products or other new initiatives pass on their way— their proponents hope—to market. There, we shone some light on how differently most large companies think about new products compared to some of their "think narrow, not broad" entrepreneurial brethren. Here in Chapter 6, we'll examine another key difference: how the necessary assets are acquired.

"Why should I invest in those assets before I know whether my new venture will pan out?" In most large companies, there's an unstated rule that many, if not all, of the assets required to pursue something new—including a physical facility, like a factory or another retail store, for example—will have to be built, leased, or bought and paid for. Investment, they call it. But why, street-smart entrepreneurs ask, in their counter-conventional fashion, should I invest in those assets before I know whether my new venture will pan out? "Wouldn't it be better if I can borrow them?" at least until things are proven, they ask. "Why put money unnecessarily at risk if I don't have to? Let's break that rule!"

There are multiple reasons that breaking the conventional rules and borrowing instead of buying the necessary assets—physical, human, whatever—to get something new underway make good sense, especially if you are working in your own business where it's you who sets the rules:

- *It manages risk*. As we've seen, every new venture—whether started around a kitchen table, in the innovation department of a large company, or in one of Amazon's two-pizza teams—is chock-a-block full of risk and uncertainty. In reality, every new venture is little more than a bundle of hypotheses that await affirmation (the proponent hopes!) or rejection. Why risk the capital if you can postpone that out-of-pocket investment until more is known?

- *It buys flexibility*. Once money is committed to a certain course of action, it's difficult to change course to a more viable Plan B. And we know from empirical evidence that most of the time, Plan A isn't quite right.[1]

- *It buys freedom and independence*. For aspiring entrepreneurs, once an investor is inside your tent, you're going to be getting lots of "advice" and "support," whether you want it or not and whether it's on-target or not. Perhaps some "dictates," too. Aren't freedom and independence two of the reasons why you're an entrepreneur in the first place?

- *It keeps more future winnings for you.* Too often these days, entrepreneurs shout "Hallelujah" when they raise their initial seed funding. Doing so, however, almost always means selling a piece of their business. Giving that stake away when risk is high means giving more of it away than if the funds are raised later, when uncertainty is reduced.

What lies ahead in Chapter 6: In the remainder of this chapter, we're going to see the stories of some audacious entrepreneurs from around the world who "borrowed" key assets they needed, sometimes at start-up, and sometimes later, to enable them to establish and sustain competitive advantage and grow. As we'll see, the mindsets you're learning in this book don't just apply at the start-up stage! If you're working in later stage start-up or in a long-established business, these lessons are for you, too.

First, we'll head for India just after India's economy opened up three decades ago and observe how Sunil Bharti Mittal and his team set about figuring how it could be possible to sell mobile phone services to impoverished rural Indian consumers at a small fraction of the price consumers elsewhere were paying. And profitably, to boot!

We'll then travel to Canada and learn how a couple of dot-com entrepreneurs got a niche e-commerce business started by borrowing pretty much everything they needed. They quickly built a business, Luxy Hair, that generated millions in profits with only a handful of employees. We'll explore how another husband-and-wife couple built a thriving outdoor adventure business in the United Kingdom, GoApe!, by "borrowing" the land and the trees on which their adventure courses were built. And the parking lots, too! On the dark side of the ledger, we'll examine the fate of Cambridge Analytica, which didn't just borrow key assets, to the tune of 50 million Facebook users' data. They took those assets without those users' permission.

Finally, we'll tie the threads together and provide some lessons about how you can bake borrowing the assets you need into your entrepreneurial mindset, and about what you can do counter-conventionally to get started to do just that. Note that borrowing the assets you need, and paying for them in one way or another, at least for a while, is completely legal. Stealing is not. Here we go!

Bharti AirTel: Selling Mobile Phone Minutes Profitably for Practically Nothing[2]

Sunil Bharti Mittal wanted to be an entrepreneur from an early age. His first venture, at age 18 in 1976, in Ludhiana, a small city in India's Punjab, made hot-forged crankshafts for bicycles, which he sold to bicycle makers. It didn't take long for Mittal to realize that manufacturing crankshafts, a commodity business with no pricing power, had little potential. And the local market was small. "It was very clear that I had to get out of Ludhiana into a much bigger place," he recalls.[3]

Moving to Mumbai (Bombay at that time), he eventually imported India's first portable generator from Suzuki in Japan. It was an epiphany. "I realized very early on that you need to tie up with some large entities—much, much larger than yourself." That's exactly what Mittal continued to do, forging deals to bring products from companies in East Asia—mainly Korea, Taiwan, and Japan—into the Indian market.

> One had to persuade these large companies, assure them that they needed to be in the Indian market," he points out. "We also had to convince them that we had a high governance structure despite being a small company and give them the comfort to join hands with us to exploit and come into the Indian market together.[4]

Mittal next brought the first push-button phones to India, followed by answering machines, fax machines, and eventually India's first mobile phones.

Opportunity Strikes

In 1992, Indian Finance Minister Manmohan Singh decreed that many of India's tightly regulated markets would open up. Mittal jumped at the opportunity this radical change would present. He asked for the results of a survey that the Indian government had commissioned to determine the market potential for mobile phones in Delhi. "It said that there would be a market for 5,000 cellular phones in Delhi," he laughed. "That was one more confirmation that these reports were silly and nonsensical, so we tore it up and threw it away."

Fortunately for Mittal, other potential bidders took the survey more seriously and lost interest in Delhi. Assembling a consortium of foreign partners, the new Bharti Tele-Ventures and its partners won the bid for Delhi. The race for dominance in mobile telephony in India was on!

Thanks to generous credit terms that the Swedish telecom equipment maker Ericsson provided, based on Bharti's partners' relationships, the company was able to build out its Delhi network and launch in 1995. Successful bids for licenses elsewhere in India followed, as did acquisitions of other operators that were struggling to grow. By the turn of the century, Bharti surpassed the 100,000-subscriber milestone.

A key element in Bharti's growth was a raft of financing by private equity firm Warburg Pincus, the International Finance Corporation (IFC), Telecom Italia, British Telecom, Singapore Telecommunications, and others, all of which saw the potential that India's chronically underserved telecom market offered. By 2002, Bharti, having plowed through $1 billion in capital, launched a successful initial public offering (IPO), raising another $172 million plus an additional $315 million in international debt over the months that followed. That's when Bharti's approach to the market got interesting.

Borrow, Don't Own

By 2003, Bharti had grouped all its license deals under its new AirTel brand and had become a major player in the Indian telecom industry, having won licenses in 15 of the 23 "circles" or regions where mobile phone operating licenses had been granted. These circles represented some 92 percent of the Indian cellular population. Bharti's market share in India was north of 20 percent.[5] Mittal recalls what he and his team had been thinking.

> If you're caught between speed and perfection, always choose speed, and perfection will follow. You never wait for perfect positioning, because in business you don't have the time; especially if you're small, you can't do it.[6]

❝The company's strategy would have to change from growth at any cost to a search for profitability. But how?❞

The fast-growing company was doubling its sales year-on-year. Continuing its rapid growth would mean moving more aggressively into rural markets, Mittal's team knew, where doing business was going to be much less efficient than in more urban areas. To compound the problem, Bharti discovered that rural users in India were using far fewer minutes, by half, compared to Western users. And competitive pressure had driven per-minute pricing to as low as 3 US cents per minute, compared to 10 cents in Europe and the United States. The company's strategy would have to change from growth at any cost to a search for profitability, by becoming the lowest cost provider. The focus henceforth would be on per-minute profit margins. But how?

In early 2004, co-managing director and CFO Akhil Gupta developed a plan. He was frustrated that every new spurt of growth called for new investment in the Bharti network—new investment in network equipment and IT hardware and software, new towers and base stations, and more. Gupta and his team decided to ask his network equipment suppliers, including Ericsson and others, and his main IT provider, IBM, to become outsourced partners, taking over the complete responsibility for keeping pace with Bharti's growth—building, maintaining, and servicing the network and the IT systems that supported it.

No longer would his team have to spend time poring over bids for new equipment that would soon prove insufficient. No longer would Bharti place orders for network equipment, computers, and such. The more than 1,000 Bharti staff currently managing its network and IT would be taken over by the vendors.

In late 2004, countering the conventional wisdom that the outsourcing boom meant Western companies' outsourcing to Eastern resources, Bharti made front-page headlines in the *Wall Street Journal* for "reverse outsourcing"—that is, by reaching agreements with IBM and three network equipment vendors, Ericsson, Nokia, and Siemens—to carry out Gupta's plan.[7] Under the network equipment deals, Bharti would pay for capacity only once it had been used by customers. IBM committed to certain IT service levels and would get a percentage of revenue.

One year later, despite various challenges that had to be ironed out on the fly, Gupta was happy. The vendors were, too. "It's one of the few examples of a win-win situation," recalls Gupta. "The vendors are relieved to see the end of "beauty parades" and are excited by the large volume commitment that Bharti was willing to make. For Bharti, at last, we have a predictable cost model."[8]

Borrowing Even More

Hardware and software weren't the only things that Bharti "borrowed." As mobile phone penetration grew, it became clear that phones could provide services that went well beyond telephone calls: grain pricing for rural users, online English classes, music and entertainment, and much more. Hewing close to its per-minute margin ethos, Bharti encouraged an open community of developers to invent apps for new services that users wanted, much as did Apple a couple of years later with its iPhone. It worked out a deal with Nortel to provide sophisticated call-center service on a per-call basis. Ingeniously, calls that could be resolved without a customer's speaking to a call center representative earned a higher fee, incentivizing Nortel to drive costs down. And, in a joint venture with two other Indian operators, it moved its towers into an independent tower company, Indus Towers Ltd.

Growth Takes Off

In the single month of February 2006, Bharti added 1.07 million subscribers, thanks in part to the more than 17,000 base stations in more than 3,300 towns that its new strategy delivered.[9] As a result of its relentless growth in subscribers, in 2008 Bharti became India's largest mobile operator. In 2009, Bharti ventured outside India for the first time, launching mobile phone service in Sri Lanka. In 2010, it bought Kuwait-based Zain Telecom's operations in 15 countries in Africa, extending its footprint to an area covering 1.8 billion people.[10]

Fast-forwarding to 2021, Bharti's revenues reached $13.5 billion, its market cap reached nearly $40 billion, and it ranked number 92 on *Forbes Magazine's* list of the world's most innovative companies.[11] "Borrowing" key assets had taken the fledgling entrepreneur from Ludhiana and his fast-growing company a very long way!

Alex Ikonn and Mimi Naghizada
Borrow It All![12]

Alex Ikonn and his fiancée, Mimi Naghizada, were preparing for their upcoming wedding. It was 2010 and the world of e-commerce was growing fast. After a disappointing experience in a nearby shopping mall in Toronto, where they lived, Mimi and her sister Leyla came home disappointed. Mimi had been wondering how to style her hair for her wedding, and she had decided that hair extensions, which numerous celebrities in the fashion magazines were wearing, might offer the solution she was after.

Alas, the packages she found cost $150 and were insufficient. But two packages contained more hair than she needed. Worse, the color selection was limited and the product quality questionable. "The issue I had," recalled Mimi, "was it just wasn't thick enough. So it didn't look natural! I cannot wear this product, and I can't even return it because it's human hair."[13] Ikonn, overhearing Mimi's and Leyla's conversation, wondered whether hair extensions sold online might be the entrepreneurial opportunity he'd been looking for.

Mimi's Problem Leads to Alex's Solution

Ikonn had been putting the social media skills he'd learned in an earlier job to work in a friend's start-up. An inquisitive sort, he was always asking questions. How did e-commerce work? What sort of resources were available for selling online, for warehousing and shipping, and more? Were there any legal impediments for a Canadian company to sell to American consumers? Intrigued by the opportunity, he logged onto the Alibaba website and began searching for hair extension suppliers. He contacted every supplier he could find, peppering them with questions via email. Quickly discovering that there were differences in responsiveness among them, he narrowed the list to a handful of Asian suppliers and requested samples.

In a matter of weeks, after seeing samples, he and Mimi were able to select a supplier whose quality seemed "Amazing," according to Mimi,[14] and whose prices seemed fair. Concurrently, Mimi and Leyla started a YouTube channel that focused on hair styling advice. They would look for the most frequent hair-related search terms on Google and look to Yahoo Answers to see what kind of hair-related questions were being asked. Benefiting from Ikonn's social media experience, they began building an online presence and seeking out and interacting with fashion and beauty personalities whenever they could.

Assembling (i.e., "Borrowing") the Resources

Meanwhile, Ikonn was figuring out how to source—that is, borrow—the various assets that their new venture would need. He built a simple (free) WordPress website that included a PayPal button for payment. He made a deal with an American logistics provider, Shipwire, to receive, hold, and ship orders as they arrived. For a few hundred dollars a month plus a few dollars for each item shipped, Shipwire would do everything. All Shipwire would need from Luxy, as their new business was going to be called, was the customers' orders and where to ship them!

❝Mustering up their courage, the couple decided to apply simultaneously for multiple credit cards that were offering zero interest for six months on cash advances.❞

Happily having secured most of the resources they would need, there remained just one challenge: financing an initial inventory of hair extensions. Mustering up their courage, the couple decided to apply simultaneously for multiple credit cards that were offering zero interest for six months on cash advances. Together with $6,000 that Ikonn's mother was willing to draw from her line of credit and lend to them, the couple was able to assemble $20,000, enough to finance the first shipment.

Getting Started

They placed the order and several weeks later, Shipwire reported that the shipment of hair extensions had arrived. Shipwire quickly sent them samples of each color. "The quality we'd hoped for is indeed there, just like the samples we saw," exclaimed Mimi, tearing into the packages. "And the colors are exactly what we wanted!"[15] By now, Mimi saw that she was beginning to be seen as something of a hair-styling expert! She and Leyla had been working hair extensions into some of the video tutorials they were shooting in Leyla's bedroom and posting on her YouTube channel. Now, they began referring their YouTube followers to the Luxy Hair website with a link, which cost them nothing, either. "Let's go live tomorrow," Ikonn shouted with glee. "Everything is in place. Our website. A quality supplier. A PayPal account. Shipwire."[16]

Luxy Hair Takes Off

There was only one question that remained: Would sales take off? They did! Week 1, $1,000; month 1, $20,000; year 1, $1 million. The even better news was that within six months, by late 2011, they were able to repay their credit card advances and Ikonn's Mom, too! Sometimes Plan A actually works! Two years on, in mid-2013, Mimi's YouTube channel had amassed 1 million subscribers and had accumulated 2.5 million views of her how-to videos and 245 million views in total.

By 2016, Luxy's own YouTube channel had won more than 300,000 subscribers and more than 250 million views. Fast-forwarding to 2019, the couple was running a highly profitable multimillion-dollar business with two additional e-commerce start-ups underway. And, having "borrowed" almost all the resources the business needed, all this had been accomplished with just 3.5 employees!

Why invest in resources when they can be borrowed? And why give up an equity stake in your business to get your hands on the capital and other resources you need? Wouldn't you prefer to make the future winnings—the value of your business and whatever profit and cash it generates—*yours*?

GoApe: Living Life Adventurously![17]

Tristram and Rebecca Mayhew were at a career and lifestyle crossroad. It was mid-2001, and, after a fast start to his post-Army career with one, and then another, large multinational company, Tristram and Rebecca had concluded that moving from London to Barcelona for a major promotion that had been offered to Tristram wasn't going to work. The arrival of their first daughter had prompted some soul-searching and they'd settled on what they really wanted going forward:

- To run their own business
- To do it from home, in order to facilitate more family time with what they hoped would be a growing family
- To be based in the countryside
- To have the business be outdoor-based, not desk-bound
- To do something they could be passionate about

Fortuitously, on a holiday trip to France that summer, they stumbled across an outdoor adventure business deep in the Auvergne national forest, Forêt de l'Aventure. "From the moment we set eyes on it," recalls Tristram, "We both thought, 'What an inspiring business.'"[18] Arriving back home in London, they got to work exploring the idea of doing something similar in the United Kingdom. They quickly discovered that there were about 400 high-ropes courses in the United Kingdom, most of which were built with telephone poles and targeted the management training and development market. None targeted ordinary consumers.

The Forêt de l'Aventure was nothing like them. It was a tree-top adventure course set 30 to 40 feet above the ground. Most of the rope walkways, ziplines, and other features were fastened in a noninvasive manner to trees, not telephone poles. Customers clipped themselves in with safety harnesses and spent a couple of hours traversing the course. It was challenging, exhilarating, and far more aesthetically attractive than the UK courses that Tristram and Rebecca had observed. "But could it be a viable business?" the couple wondered.

Tristram reached out to management at Altus, the operator of the French course. Not only did Altus have no plan to enter the United Kingdom, but they would be happy to work with others who shared their vision and values. Altus would assist.

Removing Obstacles

The Mayhews' next call was to the Royal Society for the Prevention of Accidents (RoSPA) in the United Kingdom, a 90-year-old charity whose mission was to reduce injuries and save lives by providing information, advice, resources, and training. Much to the Mayhews's surprise, RoSPA was becoming concerned that the UK government's growing emphasis on health and safety was creating a risk-obsessed culture in the United Kingdom. In RoSPA's view, people should be encouraged to live life adventurously, though not recklessly. RoSPA, too, would be supportive!

Encouraged, the couple turned to a crucial question. "Where can we build a pilot site?" A bit of online research revealed that the largest

This is the big idea that we didn't know we were looking for.

owner of woodlands in the United Kingdom was the UK Forestry Commission. Importantly, it operated 30 Forest Visitor Centres, each of them complete with parking, toilets, and refreshment facilities. Through a friend, Tristram managed to get invited to meet with the commission's East Anglian regional office with what Tristram promised would be a "recreational idea that may be of interest." "This is the big idea that we didn't know we were looking for," was the enthusiastic response following his presentation.[19] A tour of the visitor's center in the commission's Thetford Forest came next. "It has fabulous trees, 180,000 visitors per year, and all the infrastructure we need," he reported excitedly to Rebecca.[20]

Thinking ahead, and concerned with ensuring that he could gain access to other Forestry Commission sites going forward, he was able to negotiate a deal with the commission's national headquarters in Bristol. The parties agreed on a six-site deal with exclusivity for five years, until 2006. Even better, if the Mayhews opened at least five sites in the first four years, the exclusivity period would be extended to 26 years. A race against time was on!

GoApe! Is Born

On March 26, 2002, the first of what would be many GoApe! forest adventure sites opened in the Thetford Forest, with thanks to the Altus team that co-planned and built the site. There were 30 obstacles, including Tarzan swings, rope ladders and trapezes, challenging rope bridges, precarious balance beams, and speedy ziplines.

The design explicitly included elements of well-managed risk, enabling customers to "live life adventurously" at least for a few hours, according to Chief Gorilla Tristram, and enjoy the forest in an entirely new way.[21] After receiving initial training, customers clipped themselves into the safety system (reconnecting at each section of the course) and set out on their adventure.

Financing Early Growth

Eager to retain sole ownership of their fledgling venture and keep any future winnings for themselves, the couple sold a flat that Rebecca owned, generating enough proceeds to cover Thetford's £80,000 in start-up costs and then some. Soon, however, it became clear that their remaining funds and the cash flow from Thetford, which was performing well, would only finance two-and-a-half more sites. It was also clear that more hands on deck were needed if the "five sites in four years" threshold were to be achieved.

The solution? Tristram convinced a former UK Army buddy to join GoApe! as operations director. Will Galbraith would manage the construction and operation of the sites as they opened, freeing Tristram to scour the Forest Commission's forests for the most promising sites and negotiate the terms of the leases, based on a percentage of revenue they generated. Galbraith agreed to work for free for his first year and loan the business £50,000, thereby funding the anticipated shortfall for opening sites two, three, and four, in exchange for a stake in the business.

Growing Pains

Alas, Galbraith's £50,000 proved not enough. Site two at Grizedale opened on schedule in early 2003 with promising early results. But delays in getting government planning permission pushed the next opening at Moors Valley back by eight weeks, a disappointing development in what the Mayhews had learned was a seasonal business. Worse, site four, at Sherwood Pines, opened but was performing poorly. In that former coal-mining area with a troubled economy, the locals were showing little interest in taking forest adventures! In June 2003, with the peak summer season looming, the Mayhews were worried that their dream was about to go bust.

Thankfully, Tristram's mother came through with a six-week £40,000 loan to enable the business to "make payroll" at the end of June, and Galbraith made a further investment in return for more shares. Business picked up and GoApe! survived its close call, closing the 2003 year with a loss of £99,000 on revenue of £688,000 against 2002's £20,000 profit on sales of £152,000.

In 2004, thanks to a £100,000 loan from the United Kingdom's Small Firms Loan Guarantee Scheme, the company opened its fifth site in the Thames River valley. The 26-year period of exclusivity was captured, and GoApe! closed the 2004 year with a £170,000 profit on sales of £1.4 million.

Growth Achieved

Over the next 17 years, GoApe! grew relentlessly, though not always without difficulty, including an ill-fated and short-lived venture into trampoline parks (where nothing was "borrowed" and the investments required and the operating costs were substantial!) and a difficult expansion into the United States. Ingeniously, much of the growth was achieved by "borrowing" the existing sites to open "Forest Segway" sites, for people whose idea of fun didn't include high-wire adventure! They could join their friends for a GoApe! outing but keep their feet planted firmly on a Segway electric vehicle and explore the forest terrain on the ground! Then "Tree Top Junior" courses, designed for kids aged 4 to 10, followed, again using sites and terrain that were already open.

> **GoApe! was "borrowing" and reusing its own assets to generate more revenue per site, not to mention creating better career opportunities for their management team.**

GoApe! was "borrowing" and reusing its own assets to generate more revenue per site, not to mention creating better career opportunities for their management team. Recalls Rebecca, "From the beginning, we'd wanted the business to help people to "live life adventurously" and move from "I can't" to "I can." But we also wanted to create worthwhile, rewarding jobs for people who loved the outdoors and an incredibly fun-loving culture that would encourage them to stay. Now we could offer them career paths, too."[22]

In 2022, after having flirted with taking on private equity investment to grow faster, the Mayhews decided to sell the thriving business to their employees. With 33 sites in the United Kingdom, most of them featuring two or all three concepts, plus another 16 sites in the United States with a minority operating partner, GoApe! was generating sufficient cash to enable the employees to finance the deal with debt and take over the business over the ensuing five years.

Better yet, for the employee-buyers, the exclusivity deal with the Forest Commission still had six years to run. And the Mayhews walked away, albeit gradually, with a handsome return on their initial investment and the immense satisfaction that they'd lived up to the values and principles with which they'd set forth at the outset of their journey. "Borrowing" the trees and all the visitor facilities had worked out very well!

Cambridge Analytica: When "Borrowing" Crosses the Line

The British brothers Nigel and Alex Oakes polished their trade by advising dictators, helping to swing elections in Africa, leading counterterrorism operations in Afghanistan, Iraq, and Somalia, and more. "We use the same techniques as Aristotle and Hitler . . . We appeal to people on an emotional level to get them to agree on a functional level," Nigel Oakes reported, in describing their work.[23] Psycho-ops, as their craft has become known, had become a big business, with politicians from Kenya to the West Indies calling on their company SCL and its subsidiaries to attempt to influence elections through social media profiling and the use of "big data." A little more than a decade into the twenty-first century, the Oakes's and two additional partners, Alexander Nix and Mark Turnbull, spotted an opportunity to take their election division's act onto a bigger stage, the United States, via a new subsidiary called Cambridge Analytica (CA).

Robert Mercer, a major funder and supporter of Donald Trump's presidential campaign and of other conservative causes, became CA's principal shareholder. Steve Bannon, who would later become an advisor to Trump, signed on as a board member and minority investor. CA was ready to roll in what was looking to be a lucrative US market.

There was one problem. CA required enormous amounts of data to do its work, and it had no US data.

But there was one problem. CA required enormous amounts of data to do its work, and it had no US data.

Obtaining Data

A data solution arrived in the person of Christopher Wylie, a 24-year-old Canadian data junkie who was fascinated by the power of data in politics. Wylie had contacts at Cambridge University in the United Kingdom, where its Psychometrics Centre had developed tools for mapping personality traits based on what people liked on Facebook. When the Psychometrics Centre declined to work with CA, Wylie found someone who would, a Cambridge professor, Aleksandr Kogan, who knew of the techniques his colleagues had pioneered.

Kogan created a new online quiz, This Is My Digital Life, and signed up 270,000 Facebook users who were paid to participate in the quiz. Ominously and probably unnoticed by most of them, they also agreed in the fine print that their friends' Facebook data could also be pulled, to be used for "academic purposes." The result was that some 50 million profiles were obtained without permission, of which 30 million were sufficiently useful to enable CA to build psychographic profiles by matching the Facebook data to other data sources. As Wylie later acknowledged, "We wanted as much [data] as we could get. Where it came from, who said we could have it—we weren't really asking."[24] But under British data protection laws, it was strictly illegal for anyone's personal data to be sold to a third party without their consent. CA was breaking rules, and the law, too.

With plenty of US data ready to let the algorithms do their work, CA was ready to roll. Though the links between the Kogan data and the various election campaigns that followed are murky and unclear, Nix later boasted that the company ultimately ran more than 4,000 campaigns for Donald Trump in the 2016 presidential election, totaling over a billion impressions or views.

"It was the first data-driven election," he said. "It was less about politics and more about the shift in communications."[25]

A Whistle Blows

The liberal-leaning Wylie didn't take long to become uncomfortable with how his work was being used in support of the hard-right candidates that Mercer and Bannon favored. He left CA in 2014, apparently grabbing or copying a trove of documents on his way out. In March 2018, with concerns about data privacy ramping up in the United Kingdom, a consortium of newspapers from there and the United States obtained documents from Wylie that put CA under investigation and shoved Facebook into the headlines, knocking $50 billion off its market cap. Facebook denied responsibility for the theft. "This was a scam—and a fraud," said Paul Grewal, a vice president at the social network.[26]

A firestorm of negative publicity for both CA and Facebook quickly followed. Two weeks later, Facebook finally apologized. "I'm sorry we didn't do more at the time.

> **A firestorm of negative publicity for both CA and Facebook quickly followed.**

We're now taking steps to ensure this doesn't happen again," wrote Mark Zuckerberg in ads appearing in the *New York Times* and several other leading newspapers in the United States and the United Kingdom.[27] The US Federal Trade Commission imposed a $5 billion penalty and a series of privacy restrictions on Facebook in 2019,[28] and Facebook agreed to pay a £500,000 fine, the maximum allowable, to the UK's Information Commissioner's Office for its role in the scandal.[29]

Game Over for Cambridge Analytica?

For CA, it was game over, or so everyone thought. Though it continued to deny any wrongdoing, on May 2, 2018, the company started insolvency proceedings in the United States and the

United Kingdom. The scandal had left it with no clients and a mounting burden of legal fees to defend the charges against it.[30] Nix was banned from serving as a director of any UK company for seven years.

But was CA's game really over? A new British company, Emerdata, founded in 2017, with Mercer and other SCL and CA players as its directors, acquired the remains of CA and SCL and its subsidiaries prior to the 2018 insolvency proceedings. Will its methodologies and its political intent, if not the stolen data, live on? Time will tell.

Lessons Learned About "Borrowing" versus Stealing

You don't have to be an entrepreneur out on your own to "borrow" the assets you need to get a promising innovation underway. Just because most big companies assume that the initial assets should be bought or built does not mean that you can't convince your boss to let you borrow them instead. If you're fortunate, you may have a boss who values being counter-conventional as much as you do.

On the other hand, if you're a resource-starved, cash-strapped entrepreneur trying to get your start-up underway—just like Alex Ikonn and Mimi Naghizada and Tristram and Rebecca Mayhew—borrowing the assets you need is a no-brainer, in my view. Pretty much anyone can adopt this counter-conventional and highly entrepreneurial mindset. In this section of the chapter, I'll address the lessons the case studies have taught us about the variety of what you can "borrow"—not just hard assets—and some of the benefits of doing so.

On borrowing credibility: If you're starting something new within a well-established business, credibility may not be an issue for you. But for first-time entrepreneurs, credibility is a big deal. You may need credibility to land the best suppliers and to land them on attractive terms. You'll need credibility to convince customers that you will deliver what you promise, as you saw in the Bharti AirTel case study. The presence of Bharti's respected global partners convinced Ericsson to give it generous credit terms from the outset. Having engaged with the French Forêt de l'Aventure and RoSPA probably gave Tristram Mayhew credibility in his initial dealings with the UK Forestry Commission, too.

On borrowing expertise: We saw how Tristram Mayhew convinced Will Galbraith to come on board as Operations Director, "borrowing" Galbraith's first year of employment without pay and freeing Mayhew to scour other Forestry Commission sites. Mayhew "borrowed" Altus' expertise to plan and build the first GoApe! sites as well. Earlier in this book, in Chapter 2, you saw how Arnold Correia, in addition to "borrowing" the satellite capacity he needed, "borrowed" Herbe Zambrone's expertise to help make SubWay Link's ambitious pivot into Corporate TV a successful one.

On transforming your business model: "Borrowing" the assets you need, at any stage of your journey, can transform your company's business model, as Bharti AirTel did in order to profitably serve India's rural customers. For GoApe!, negotiating a deal whereby rent for its Forestry Commission sites was paid as a percentage of revenue—thus in arrears!—not only gave its lower-volume sites a chance to be profitable, but also vastly improved its return on investment.

To be sure, GoApe! had to equip each new site with its high-wire adventure apparatus, to the tune of around £100,000 for each site, but it didn't have to buy land (nor lease it with a heavy deposit, as was the custom for such leases in the United Kingdom; nor restrooms, nor parking lots, either). Limiting the initial investment meant that each typical site would pay back its initial investment in as little as two years. Thereafter, each two years' cash flow could be used to fund an additional site. The result? GoApe! became a customer-funded growth machine.[31] Who needs investors when you've got a business model like theirs? "Borrowing" the assets your venture needs, instead of investing in them, is a rule well worth breaking, it seems!

Similarly, Alex Ikonn's creativity in outsourcing virtually every activity that his and Mimi's hair extension business required has meant that he and Mimi have been able to own and operate a sizeable business with only a few employees. There are hardly any fixed costs in Luxy's model, so it can be profitable at almost any level of sales.

On the benefits of speed: Most of the time, borrowing the assets you need is much faster than having to build them. And, when you're innovating something new, speed matters. LinkedIn founder Reid Hoffman puts it this way:

> There's a bunch of things that, structurally, start-ups have as advantages over big companies. One is speed across all levels. It's not just speed at raw execution. But it's also speed of hiring, speed of decisioning, speed of learning, speed of judgment of product-market fit, etc. . . . They [big companies] have a group consensus process, so that if they're going to take a risk, somebody who's in a managerial or executive role will question that risk. So it's hard for them to do, hard to move quickly.[32]

The Luxy Hair founders got their business up and running fast by borrowing pretty much everything they needed. Sunil Bharti Mittal won the Delhi mobile telephony license in part because speed was central to how Mittal operated and in part because he was able to assemble a consortium of foreign partners quickly, due to the fact that he'd been doing just that for many years. Speed matters, indeed!

On whether to pay or not to pay—and *when and how* to pay: I hasten to note that "borrowing" assets—whether human or otherwise—often means you don't fork over any cash for them up front: the first year of Galbraith's time at GoApe!, for example; Alex Ikonn getting most of his start-up capital by taking out six-month interest-free loans on new credit cards; Mimi Naghizada's YouTube channel.

If you can obtain the assets your business needs without paying cash for them, at least up front, all the better. But more typically such assets get paid for one way or another. GoApe! gave Galbraith some equity in the company and paid percentage rent for the use of its Forest Commission sites. Bharti Airtel paid its network equipment suppliers and IBM for the outsourced equipment and IT services they delivered. So paying is fine, if you must. Paying later is finer!

On seeking win-win deals: You might think you will have to beg to be able to "borrow" the assets you need. But no, not always. The UK Forestry Commission was thrilled to have GoApe! bring more people to its sites. Similarly, as we saw in Bharti Air Tel's deals with its equipment suppliers, there were benefits on both sides of those transactions, too. Bharti transformed its business model, and its vendors locked in a fast-growing customer's business for the long term. My experience tells me that vendors want long-term deals and are often willing to think out-of-the-box to secure them. So don't be afraid to ask!

On the downside, as we saw with Cambridge Analytica, stealing what you need—Facebook user data, taken without its users' permission—can have negative implications, not only for the one who steals the assets, but for others who may be unaware of what's really going on. Facebook did not steal its users' data, but it failed to adequately protect it, to be sure. The financial and reputational damage it incurred was substantial.

Bonus Lessons Learned

This chapter's lessons about borrowing the assets you need are crucially important, whether at start-up or in a company of greater size that wants to grow or grow faster. But there are additional lessons the Mayhews' journey holds, as well.

On the value of exclusivity: GoApe!'s 26-year exclusive deal with the UK Forestry Commission would not have happened without Tristram Mayhew having thought ahead about how best to build a business whose business model could grow and how to maintain attractive profit margins. Keeping prospective competitors from bidding against him for future Forest Commission sites was a stroke of genius. You should try to do likewise whenever you can. It will help you keep competition at bay!

On building *your* company's culture: If you're in the mortuary business, it might not be easy to build the kind of playful, employee-first, fun-loving culture that makes GoApe!'s employees love coming to work each day and feel a sense of belonging. A title like Mayhew's Chief Gorilla for a mortuary CEO just wouldn't fit. Chief Hole-Digger? Probably not.

But in most services businesses, putting your employees first means, in turn, that they are more likely to treat your customers well. We've all had customer experiences in services businesses where that's clearly not the case. Such a culture can be a crucial differentiator in industries in which entry barriers are low or your competitors promise good service but fail to deliver it. We saw Simon Cohen do just that in the freight forwarding industry in Chapter 3.

The global coronavirus pandemic appears to have led many workers toiling away in jobs they didn't love to rethink what they want out of their work. If you're able to create the kind of culture that Tristram and Rebecca Mayhew have created, it will serve you—and your customers—very well.[33]

How to Add "Borrowing Your Assets" to *Your* Entrepreneurial Mindset

In one of the businesses I started after leaving the big-company world many years ago, a small chain of stores that sold fresh pasta and sauces and related products to take home, we needed a commercial kitchen in which to prepare the sauces and sheets of fresh pasta—which would be shipped fresh daily to our stores and custom-cut to the customer's wishes before their eyes: linguine, tagliarini, fettuccine, or angel hair.

Did we build one? Nope, at least not at the outset. We found a gourmet food store whose kitchen was busy during the day but empty at night. We "borrowed" that kitchen, through the opening of our first four stores, to build our confidence in our retail concept. That saved us a lot of cash that we were able to put into opening those first few stores. With those stores and a spanking new commissary eventually up and running, we were then able to raise additional capital to fund further growth, on attractive terms.

If you're working on your own venture, rather than in a deep-pocketed large company, you may well need to raise capital at some point. You'll raise that capital more easily, and on better terms, if you can demonstrate progress, of course. But "borrowing" the initial assets you need demonstrates something else, too. It shows that you're conscious of and serious about running a capital-efficient business. Investors like that! A lot!

As the noted VC investor Bruce Golden of Accel puts it,

> One of the great things about being an owner/founder is that you build a business, you own ideally most of it and you try and preserve that ownership over time. And the key way to achieve that is through capital efficiency. The venture model is really based on the idea that as a business progresses and as it achieves milestones, that raises the probability of success. (So) you are able to raise capital at

different stages. In essence, sell smaller slices of the business for more capital. And so, at the heart of this notion is capital efficiency. Capital is expensive, and entrepreneurs early on should really understand just how vital it is to get their arms around building a capital efficient business. So we look for businesses that are inherently capital efficient because generally they are more successful over time, the teams are more conservative and healthier, and, you know, just grow up in an environment where they spend money really effectively."[34]

So, what should *you* do now to make "borrowing"—instead of investing—a central pillar in *your* own entrepreneurial mindset? This one's easy. As the Nike TV commercials used to say, "Just do it!" For every asset you need—physical, human, financial, whatever—to get your innovation or your new venture underway, ask yourself how you can get your hands on it without investing up front. Doing so will bring you most if not all the benefits I've outlined here: a better business model, speed to market, credibility, expertise, capital efficiency and more. Just. Do. It!

Closing Thoughts

Of the six counter-conventional mindsets revealed in this book, this one is the easiest to adopt. It works inside large companies. It works for start-ups. It works for most any kind of personality. It works anywhere in the world. In any kind of business: services or products; B2B, or B2C. So what are you waiting for? Break that big-company rule that says investment comes first. Borrow—but don't steal—the assets you need and get your journey underway!

7

What Entrepreneurs Can Do That Big Companies Can't: Instead of Asking Permission, Beg Forgiveness Later

Instead of asking permission, beg forgiveness later

Yes, we can!

Beg, borrow, (but don't steal)

Your counter-conventional mindset

Problem-first, not product-first logic

Ask for the cash, ride the float

Think narrow, not broad

As you saw at the outset of Chapters 4 and 6, many large companies have well-established procedures for getting new initiatives underway and for funding the investment required. Apart from determining whether the opportunity is attractive and seeking the requisite capital to fund something new, those procedures often require an examination of the external environment to determine some other parameters, too. Is the venture legal? Are there regulations that might limit or forbid it? Are there risks, including some perhaps previously unseen, that should be considered?

Fortunately, in such companies, there are committees of all kinds and armies of lawyers whose main job is to protect the company from those unseen risks, avoid potential lawsuits, and keep its executives out of jail. Why? Many companies' leaders, at their core, don't like risk very much. They prefer as much certainty as they can get their hands on. If the company is listed on a stock exchange, they feel obliged to deliver the earnings that investors expect and deliver them consistently, quarter to quarter. No down quarters, please.

Similarly, in many business schools, there's coursework in business law so that graduates better understand what they can and cannot do. There are courses in business ethics, to encourage graduates to think not just about the letter of the law, but about the difference between right and wrong, though what's seen as right and wrong ethically can vary from place to place around the world and from one culture to another.[1]

The result of all this thinking and of the bureaucratic cholesterol that often accompanies it, in many established companies, is threefold:

1. There are lots of people, processes, and perspectives that can say "no" to a new initiative.
2. There are few who have the authority to say "yes."
3. And, whatever the verdict, it rarely arrives quickly.

Often, however, the pursuit of opportunity requires acting quickly, as we were reminded by Sunil Bharti Mittal in Chapter 6. "Who knows," wonder most entrepreneurs, "Who else in another garage is thinking about doing the same thing?" Speed to market can matter—sometimes a lot!

If you're working on a new initiative that breaks some of your big company's conventional rules, you're probably well versed in the phenomenon I've just pointed out.

> **Most big companies simply can't move forward in the face of legal or regulatory ambiguity.**

For you, sad to say, this chapter's advice may not be very applicable. The reality is that most big companies simply can't move forward in the face of legal or regulatory ambiguity. But if you're an entrepreneur unencumbered by such barriers, you can, as you'll see in this chapter!

Any entrepreneur seeking to do business in a regulated setting should, of course, ask, "Is my idea legal?" As we'll see in this chapter, sometimes the law or the applicable regulatory frameworks simply haven't addressed what an entrepreneur wants to do, typically when it's something that's not been done before, at least not in the same way. Sometimes, as we'll also see, one law might conflict with others. Which one might rule? Sometimes laws, especially laws written a long time ago when conditions were different, simply aren't enforced, perhaps because they make little sense today.

It's these kinds of legally ambiguous circumstances that we address in this chapter. Instead of waiting for a clear answer to the "Is it legal?" question, many successful entrepreneurs faced with legal or regulatory ambiguity have learned to simply forge ahead. Asking permission, after all, would have two likely downsides:

- It could retard speed to market.
- The answer, once the legal advisors or regulators think about it, might turn out to be "Not a good idea." That's not what any eager entrepreneur wants to hear.

And, who knows? It might be that begging forgiveness after the fact will turn out not to be necessary! Thus, as we'll see in this chapter, a better course of action, in many entrepreneurs' minds, is never to ask permission at all. Just get the ball rolling, and if the venture eventually runs into legal or regulatory challenges, they'll beg forgiveness later, contritely of course, and seek to resolve them at that time. Meanwhile, if the venture pans out, they may have won an abundance of customers who love what they do and may join the venture in pleading that any legal ambiguity be resolved in their favor.

What's next in Chapter 7: We'll open the chapter with the story of Travis Kalanick, the audacious, pugnacious co-founder and first CEO of Uber, the upstart disruptor that, alongside Uber's many imitators, has changed how people get around in big cities worldwide, to many consumers' delight but to some regulators' chagrin. We'll then travel to India and read how two plucky entrepreneurs, Manish Sabharwal and Ashok Reddy, decided that "putting India to work" was a sufficiently noble cause to skip asking for permission and get on with the business, despite a warning from their attorney that they could end up in jail.

Then we'll close with the case study of Josephine, a California start-up that enabled cooks to sell meals prepared in their home kitchens to others. For Josephine, violating the food-safety regulations didn't work out very well. And, as always, we'll wrap up with some lessons learned about how you can incorporate never asking permission into *your* entrepreneurial mindset.

To be perfectly clear at the outset, encouraging aspiring entrepreneurs to be lawbreakers is **not** what this chapter is about. Break the conventional rules, as you've seen throughout this book? Sure. Break the law? No.

Travis Kalanick: Visionary Disruptor, Bare-Knuckled Brawler, or Unethical Scoundrel?[2]

It was a snowy night in Paris in 2008. Two American entrepreneurs, Garret Camp and Travis Kalanick, were visiting the City of Light to attend an annual European tech conference, LeWeb. Both men had recently sold their previous ventures and were on the hunt for their next entrepreneurial gig. But it's not easy to catch a cab on a snowy night in Paris, they discovered. As they discussed start-up ideas with a roomful of entrepreneurs the next day, the idea of an on-demand ride-hailing service app arose, among many others.

Back in San Francisco afterwards, Camp was sufficiently enthralled with the idea that he bought the online domain name UberCab.com. He wanted Kalanick to be his partner. Why? Camp recalled that, while climbing the Eiffel Tower together, Kalanick had jumped over barriers to get a better view of the city arrayed below. "I liked that quality of going for it. I knew such a big idea would take a lot of guts, and he impressed me as someone who had that."[3]

The duo launched the beta version of UberCab in San Francisco in May 2010, with a handful of drivers with fancy black cars and a small seed round of capital. Anyone could download the app, enter their credit card info, press a button, and *Voilà!* a car would magically come pick them up. As Camp described it, "Everyone could ride like a millionaire."[4] In October, however, both the San Francisco Municipal Transportation Agency and the California Public Utilities Commission issued cease-and-desist orders. Among other things, the authorities objected to the use of "cab" in UberCab's name, since the company had neither applied for nor obtained a taxi license.

The pugnacious Kalanick had exactly what he wanted—a public fight. "We're totally legal, like totally legal, and the government is telling us to shut down. And you can either do what they say, or you can fight for what you believe,"[5] recalled Kalanick, setting a pattern of what he called "principled confrontation" that would drive the company forward. He and Camp simply ignored most of the orders, but they did change the company's name to Uber.

Controversy Pays Off

Playing the victim of government overreach in the business press gave Uber visibility, and money soon followed. In February 2011, Benchmark Capital invested $10 million, valuing the fledgling company at $60 million. "I had this idea of looking at a smartphone as a remote control for real life, and this was the best example I had ever seen," said Benchmark's Matt Cohler. Additional rounds followed, round after round, at ever higher valuations. By the summer of 2014, the four-year-old Uber had reached a valuation of $17 billion.

In one city after another, Uber would simply enter, typically without bothering to ask the local regulator whether the Uber model would fly from a regulatory perspective. As a result, Uber found itself engaging in a long-running battle with the taxi industry and its regulators who Kalanick claimed were in its pocket. "I think of them as robber barons," says Barry Korngold, president of the San Francisco Cab Drivers Association, about Uber. "They started off by operating illegally, without following any of the regulations and unfairly competing. And that's how they became big—they had enough money to ignore all the rules."[6]

Kalanick saw things differently and had little interest in any compromise. "If you don't agree with the core principles . . . then you have to have what I call principled confrontation," he says. "And so that is the thing that we do that I think can rub some people the wrong way." But Uber was rubbing more than just the regulators the wrong way.

Discontent Arises

During a snowstorm in New York in 2013, Uber's surge pricing model raised rates as much as eightfold, attracting negative press and a customer backlash. Kalanick fought back. "You want supply to always be full, and you use price to basically either bring more supply on or get more supply off, or get more demand in the system or get some demand out. It's classic Econ 101."[7] Then in October 2014, as Uber cut it drivers' pay in an effort to compete on price with its US rival Lyft, Uber drivers protested, picketing and shutting off the app and refusing to serve customers. Kalanick's tone-deaf public statement the previous May that driverless cars would someday eliminate the need for drivers hadn't exactly endeared him to his driver community.

Uber's Ethics Go South

In late 2014, Uber entered Portland, Oregon, without seeking a permit, of course, as was its norm. The local regulators were not pleased. To build a case against Uber, city staffers began posing as riders seeking a ride, in hopes of taking rides with drivers who were not commercially licensed, a violation of the city's rules. But Uber had built a tool called Greyball that used app data, social media profiles of city officials, and other means to identify those who were trying to crack down on Uber. It would serve up a fake version of the app, populated with phantom cars, and cancel any rides that real Uber drivers accepted.

The city escalated, suing Uber for operating an "illegal, unregulated transportation service."[8] Chastened, Uber agreed that it would suspend its operations for three months, during which the city would find a way to make Uber's operation legal in Portland, which it did starting April 30, 2015. But what about Kalanick's self-described "principled confrontation" you may ask? What's "principled" about running the Greyball scheme in Portland and in numerous other cities around the world? Was it legal? Not clear, as observers disagreed. Ethical? No!

The Controversies Continue

Uber's win in Portland, though not without compromise, belied the nonstop controversies that followed. Numerous female riders reported being harassed. There were allegations of widespread sexual harassment within the Uber organization, too. Incredibly, Uber's executives even hatched a plan to dig up dirt on the private lives of reporters whose coverage of Uber was critical. The response was furious. "They wanted to go after my family," wrote *PandoDaily* reporter Sarah Lacy. "I've been in the valley for 20 years. This is not normal."[9] But the aggressive, combative Uber culture that Kalanick had created continued unabated.

In February 2017, Kalanick was captured on video in an explosive rant with an Uber driver over whether the company had slashed its drivers' pay. The video went viral. Kalanick issued a public apology, saying, "By now I'm sure you've seen the video where I treated an Uber driver disrespectfully. To say that I am ashamed is an extreme understatement . . . It's clear this video is a reflection of me—and the criticism we've received is a stark reminder that I must fundamentally change as a leader and grow up."[10]

But key investors on Uber's board had had enough. By mid-June, the board demanded Kalanick's resignation. He first agreed to take an indefinite leave of absence, and then, suddenly, on June 20, 2017, he was out. "I have accepted a group of investors' request to step aside, so that Uber can go back to building rather than be distracted with another fight," he wrote.[11]

Making Amends

In September 2017, London's transport authority, Transport for London (TfL) announced that it would not renew Uber's operating license, saying the company was not "fit and proper" to operate in the city, which had become Uber's largest market among the 700 cities in which it operated. The city's traditional "black cab" industry had been vocal in campaigning against the American upstart that was taking market share fast.

Uber's new CEO, Dara Khosrowshahi, a former executive at Expedia.com, quickly posted a plea on Twitter to let the company make things right. "Dear London: we r far from perfect but we have 40k licensed drivers and 3.5mm Londoners depending on us. Pls work w/us to make things right," the tweet said.[12] Some 35,000 Londoners signed a petition to London Mayor Sadiq Khan to allow Uber to continue to operate. Following an appeal of TfL's decision, Khosrowshahi and his team were eventually able to smooth the ruffled feathers and keep Uber operating.

Does Hubris Pay?

Kalanick's hubris and his strategy of simply entering new cities without asking regulators for permission and later resolving whatever problems arose, together with the abundant capital that its investors have provided, has enabled Uber to grow relentlessly. Its revenue in 2021 was more than double that of 2017, when Khosrowshahi took the reins.[13] It invented the on-demand ride-hailing industry, which millions of consumers worldwide have learned to love—and from which some 5 million Uber drivers earn part or all of their livelihoods today.

But aggressive expansion with a legally ambiguous business model need not be accompanied by an aggressive and misogynous culture internally. It need not be enabled by ethically dubious practices such as Greyball. Kudos to Kalanick for his and Camp's vision and ambition and for revolutionizing how people get around in cities worldwide. But not for his leadership style—nor for his ethics, either—which proved badly flawed. Utterly unacceptable, most observers would agree, in the twenty-first century. Was Kalanick a visionary disrupter? A bare-knuckled brawler? And/or an unethical scoundrel? I'll leave that conclusion to you.

> **Aggressive expansion with a legally ambiguous business model need not be accompanied by an aggressive and misogynous culture internally.**

Putting India to Work[14]

It was a Friday afternoon in Bangalore in 2002. Manish Sabharwal rang his longtime friend and former business partner, Ashok Reddy. "Ashok," he said, "I've got another idea with a lot of potential, but it's not entirely legal. Are you ready for a challenge?"[15]

Fifteen months earlier, the duo had sold their first start-up, India Life, which administered retirement programs for multinational companies (MNCs) operating in India, for a tidy sum. As part of the deal, Sabharwal agreed to move to Singapore and remain with the acquiring company for one year, after which the balance of the purchase price was to be paid. Before long, he found himself trapped in the stifling bureaucracy found in many MNCs.

> An environment where anybody could say no and nobody could say yes just drove me crazy. But the absolute worst part was how I had to relinquish control of the only thing I loved—dealing with the customers. In my new role, I had my ass to the customer. I wanted out.[16]

An Opportunity Beckons

At India Life, a few clients had suggested a need for a staffing provider that would take nonpermanent staff—part-time customer service or salespeople, contract workers, and the like—off their payrolls. The staffing firm would then "sell" these workers back to the company as temporary staff. This would allow the clients to make an accounting change that classified temporary workers as an expense, ultimately improving the employee productivity ratios that they reported to their home offices. This was window dressing, to be sure, but apparently important to the local country managers. Hiring temps would bring other benefits, too, including the opportunity to "road test" new hires and the flexibility to quickly add people for seasonal peaks and when business expands, and trim payrolls when business falls off.

Sabharwal was intrigued by the opportunity, and by the typical business model in the temporary staffing industry. Client companies would provide the cash at payday

❝Client companies would provide the cash at payday from which the temping firm would "make payroll."❞

from which the temping firm would "make payroll." But benefits and taxes didn't have to be paid until several weeks later. This meant that the temping firm could "ride the float" on those amounts and use that cash to fund growth, as we saw in Chapter 5. Sabharwal was also intrigued by the positive social impact of helping to create jobs in India, if temporary jobs could be used as a route into full-time employment. With clients seemingly eager, might he and Reddy bring the temporary staffing model, which was well established in Europe and elsewhere, to India at scale?

But Would It Be Legal?

Sabharwal and Reddy already knew there was a thicket of labor laws in India, more than 25,000 of them, some at the state or local level, oth-

❝There was a thicket of labor laws in India, more than 25,000 of them.❞

ers nationally. The Contract Labour Regulations Act (CLRA) of 1971 and the Industrial Disputes Act (IDA) of 1956 were the most relevant.

The main aspect of the CLRA that would be relevant to their proposed business revolved around the classification of core versus noncore work. The CLRA prohibited contract labor if (a) the process or work performed by contract labor was core to the company or (b) if the process or work being performed was of a perennial nature. Classifying the work as core and/or perennial was left for interpretation by the local or state government.

Another section of the CLRA complicated the responsibility for providing temporary workers' benefits by defining the "principal employer" as the entity where the temp was working, not the temporary staffing company that employed the temp. Many of the existing but small-scale temporary staffing companies in India, however, assumed responsibility for employee benefits and removed this liability from clients. However, this positioning seemed to defy the provisions of the CLRA.

The IDA's relevance involved the worker's right to become permanent. After a certain period of employment, anyone who worked more than a certain number of continuous days for a given employer had the right to a permanency claim. The duration of continuous employment was set at the local level and ranged between 90 and 240 days. For example, a temporary worker employed on a six-month contract, after 90 days on the job, could, under the IDA, claim for permanent employment and subsequently receive all the benefits entitled to a permanent employee, including the right to remain in her job after the temporary period expired. Was this a risk worth taking, Sabharwal and Reddy wondered.

There were other laws, too, that further complicated matters. Many of them had evolved over time in order to protect workers; some were in direct conflict with previous laws or the laws of bordering states. This lack of consistency in labor regulations made life difficult for Indian companies. Exasperated, Sabharwal fumed, "In order to comply with 100% of the labor regulations, you have to break 20% of them!"[17]

Reddy wasn't as concerned.

You're right, but remember, the exciting thing about India is there are so many ways to bend the rules. There are things we do every day that are illegal in principle, but that doesn't mean that people don't—or shouldn't—do them. Remember what St. Augustine taught us: An unjust law is no law at all.[18]

They decided to consult a trusted attorney with whom they had worked at India Life to get another perspective. The reply? "What you are proposing may be illegal and you could go to jail."[19]

Getting Started

Despite the regulatory concerns, Sabharwal and Reddy founded TeamLease in late 2002. The current labor laws were hurting India more than they were helping, in their view. Asking permission was out of the question.

> **The current labor laws were hurting India more than they were helping, in their view. Asking permission was out of the question.**

Given the regulatory ambiguity, they decided to embark on an ambitious pan-India strategy from the outset. Investing $1 million of their proceeds from the India Life sale, they opened offices in five Indian cities on day 1. Ten former India Life employees joined the founding team, and 19 more joined within a few months, thereby leveraging for TeamLease their India Life client relationships.

Aware that transaction sizes were likely to be modest, due to the much lower wages paid in India than in the already developed Western markets for temporary staff, and expecting profit margins to be to be razor-thin, the duo decided to invest heavily in IT. An automated system conducted preliminary screening on job applicants. A database captured their details such as skills, training, and location, to match against client needs. Such systems, they believed, would be a competitive differentiator and would help keep costs down.

The underlying logic of the strategy was that TeamLease, if it could grow fast enough, would become so big—and would be putting enough Indians to work—that it would be unpalatable for any government agency to risk shutting TeamLease down. But investing to grow rapidly was only one element of a two-pronged effort to insulate their company from legal challenges.

The other was to become active in public policy circles and play a leading role in advocating for labor market reforms that would "Put India to work." "Let's convert it into a battle for ideas," said Sabharwal.[20]

Sabharwal quickly emerged as the public face of the company. He established relationships with national and state politicians to spread awareness about the need to create jobs in India. He wrote articles for newspapers, which helped bring positive press to the company. TeamLease organized conferences and published comprehensive annual reports on the state of India's labor market.

The fight to change India's labor laws for the better was on, and TeamLease was at the forefront. Meanwhile, Reddy focused his energies on building relationships with a growing roster of MNC and Indian clients. A third co-founder, Mohit Gupta, ran the IT back-end and operations.

Doubling Down

In 2004 and again in 2005, the fast-growing company found itself short of cash, as TeamLease had yet to reach breakeven. Sabharwal and Reddy decided to once again fund the company's cash requirements with their own money, upping their cumulative commitment to nearly US$4 million. Reddy explained why. "We chose not to take an external investor because we knew it was a long-term opportunity and did not want money with an expiry date. Our India Life venture taught us that you can't take 5-year money on a 10-year opportunity."[21]

By March 2005, TeamLease had more than 12,000 temps on its payroll, up fivefold over the prior year's figure. And, improbably, no material challenges had arisen from government authorities. Putting India to work—and paying the requisite payroll taxes—was turning out to be in the governments' interests, too.

> **Putting India to work—and paying the requisite payroll taxes—was in the governments' interests, too.**

The rapid growth of TeamLease continued, though not without challenges. Foremost among them was finding qualified workers. With India's low literacy rate and its inadequate education system, the number of employable people was always scarce. As Sabharwal put it, "We view ourselves as a people supply chain company but we're a supply chain company running out of inventory."[22] Difficulties arose matching qualified candidates with jobs on offer. "There's a matching problem which is connecting demand to supply. There's a kid in Durgapur and a job in Calcutta," Sabharwal explained.[23]

An Acquirer Comes Knocking

India's economy was on a roll and the rapid growth of Team-Lease and its visibility had not gone unnoticed by the large multinational temporary staffing firms. In the summer of 2005, out of nowhere, a large European player made an offer to buy TeamLease for a sum that would make the TeamLease founders very wealthy. Reddy, who had spent time earlier in his career in investment banking, called one of his past I-banker colleagues. The advice? "Hedge your bets. Take the money while it's on the table."[24]

He and Sabharwal then put the question to their management team. Everyone disagreed. Reddy put it simply. "When you are having fun, it's too soon to sell. We knew we would turn profitable soon, and we were the strongest player."[25] When asked whether it might be more prudent to take a "bird in hand," he replied, "I'd rather have two birds at a later stage!"[26]

The Rest of the Story

In 2008, TeamLease passed the 80,000 temps mark and became India's number two private employer. In 2010, in an effort to better deal with the talent shortage it faced, TeamLease bought an education and training company, the Indian Institute of Job

Training. In 2016, the company IPO'd on the Bombay Stock Exchange, selling 28 percent of the company for $65 million. The company's share of the proceeds provided additional capital for the ensuing stages in the TeamLease journey. By October 2021, five years on from the IPO, its stock price had more than quadrupled. Two birds, or even a flock of birds, indeed!

What about Sabharwal's goal of reforming India's labor laws, you might wonder?

> The biggest question I have in public policy now is how do you get something done in government when everybody who matters in government agrees with you. When I was younger, I thought they disagreed with me, and I didn't have access. Now I have access and they agree with me. The reforms have done a wonderful job in creating growth, but the rising tide does not lift the leaky boats. The leaky boats need education, employment, and employability"[27]

Has TeamLease been successful in putting India to work? Indeed, it has! TeamLease has hired more than 3 million workers since its inception, more than 90 percent of whom have remained employed.[28] Had Sabharwal sought permission at the outset of the TeamLease journey, would this progress have been made? You be the judge.

Josephine's Home Cooking[29]

What if you could buy delicious take-out food from your neighbors, home-cooked, fresh from their kitchens? That's what Josephine.com co-founders Tal Safran and Charley Wang introduced in California's East Bay community, across the bay from San Francisco, in 2014. The duo focused their early efforts on understanding their two core constituencies—cooks and customers. They rented a small house in Oakland and began experimenting. Take-out or eat-in? What kinds of food would customers want? What kinds of cooks, if any, would want to cook for others?

It soon became apparent that Josephine would empower mostly low-income cooks—typically women, immigrants, and people of color—to become entrepreneurs, and would provide their time-pressed neighbors access to an incredible diversity of interesting and healthy food. Both customers and cooks relished the opportunity, and the experience, too! Renee McGhee, a 59-year old grandmother of nine, cooked every Thursday—lasagna one week, pulled pork the next—while she babysat her grandson. One friendly couple, regular patrons of McGhee's home cooking, sometimes brought a bottle of wine to share. "It was like family," she recalls.[30]

Before launching, the Josephine team already knew that food was a regulated business. Wang recalled,

> I had already read up on the history and journey of the cottage food bill. We already knew that we'd be changing and fighting a regulatory model at some point in the business. That was a really exciting opportunity to us—we knew that removing the regulatory barrier for home cook entrepreneurs would further our mission on a much larger scale than the business itself would.[31]

Some 42 US states had laws in place that permitted in-home preparation and sale of some kinds of food. In California, the Homemade Food Act of 2012 specified that such practices were only allowed for food that was safe at room temperatures—cookies, candies, snack foods, granola, jams, and the like. Dairy and meat were excluded. Permits were required, through a somewhat burdensome and costly process. Annual sales for such a home business were limited to $50,000. Do you see any legal ambiguity here? I do not.

Raising Seed Capital

Across the bay in San Francisco, Airbnb and Uber had already proven a model whereby it was possible to get a legally ambiguous business started and grow it dramatically before having to engage with regulators. Matt Jorgensen, who joined the Josephine team as a third co-founder in early 2015, recalls,

> Our early investors were not very concerned. I think they felt like we were going to have at least the same amount of time that Airbnb had had to deal with some of the regulatory issues and probably a lot longer because the sharing economy was already getting normalized and there'd be less fear. There's very much a mentality of disrupt first and figure out the regulatory context later.[32]

An early investor, Josh Miller, corroborated this view. "We'll eventually have to lead a movement and campaign around food policy and why it is outdated and needs to change—much like Uber and Airbnb have done."[33]

The Regulators Pounce

A letter to Josephine on October 27, 2015 from the City of Berkeley Environmental Health Division was the first strike. Alameda County followed a day later with a letter as well. The two authorities requested a meeting on November 4, to discuss with Josephine "apparent violations of state law." The Josephine team was expected to make an appearance. The City of Berkeley letter also formally requested the names, street addresses, and email and phone contact information of all cooks in Berkeley who had offered food for sale through the Josephine.com website.

Not long after the meeting, at which the city and county made clear their displeasure with Josephine, the county began making house calls delivering cease-and-desist letters to

Josephine's cooks. McGhee, one of the cooks to whom a letter had been delivered, was astonished. "I don't understand why I can't do what I love for people who love what I do."[34] Then, in early 2016, more Josephine cooks were slapped with cease-and-desist orders. The company responded by pausing its local operations, but it hadn't given up.

Fighting back, Jorgensen took on the government relations role and hired Airbnb's local lobbyist. He prepared arguments about how Josephine was addressing food safety issues, supporting low-income entre-

> **He learned his first government-relations lesson: The regulators enforced laws; they didn't make them or change them.**

preneurs, providing healthy food access, and more. But the city and county regulators turned a deaf ear. "There was a lot of fear on their part that they would be a famous national case if they didn't take action on something that was now very public," Jorgensen recalls. He learned his first government-relations lesson: The regulators enforced laws; they didn't make them or change them.

> They were like referees, and they saw us as a threat to them missing a call that they should be making. And so very quickly in the end of 2015, we realized our strategy needed to focus on asking elected officials to slow down. It was also becoming apparent that we might need to potentially change the law at the state level because they just kept saying, "You know, our job is to just enforce the state law and our read is that what you're doing isn't compliant with state law.[35]

Jorgensen sought support from other officials in the economic, workforce development, city council, and mayor's offices.

> Those folks were overwhelmingly concerned with helping the folks that we were working with and loved the

model. They tended to either not even understand that it was a legal gray area or believe that that was not going to be a huge problem given the impact. The reaction of elected officials was always very, very positive and with a[n] "I can't believe this isn't already legal!" reaction.[36]

The law couldn't be changed by the cities, though—it had to be changed at the state level by the California legislature.

An Effort to Change the Law

In January 2016, Jorgensen, in collaboration with a sympathetic state legislator, developed and submitted draft legislation to the California legislature. It proposed to expand the Homemade Food Act. "We thought," Jorgensen recalls, "This is armor, because it's proving we can do the right thing."[37] The bill was broad and simple. It would permit anyone to sell almost anything cooked at home.

But alarm bells rang. Justin Malan represented the Environmental Health Directors from 62 state jurisdictions in California. He imagined the risks of improperly handled raw sushi. He thought about home cooks who might come home from the grocery store with raw chicken, get distracted by something else, and then rerefrigerate it after hours on the kitchen counter. "It had none of these food safety requirements that we require of even the smallest restaurants, even the cappuccino cart," Malan says.[38] He filed a brief opposing the bill immediately, and others chimed in. "Sharing is great," said Sarah Desmond, the executive director of Housing Conservation Coordinators, "but not every law is 'outdated' just because it gets between a startup's CEO and his payday."[39]

A Change of Focus

As might have been expected, the wheels of government turned slowly. In the summer of 2016, with the proposed bill mired in committee, the Josephine team decided to switch its focus to

Seattle, Denver, and Portland, despite the presence of similar legislation there. This time, the team decided to be open with the regulators up front. "In our push to (new) markets, we've been proactive about reaching out to local regulators and officials— really getting to know people who have been in those markets for a long time who are experts and have relationships, and leaning on those to navigate," Wang recalled.[40] But resistance arose there, too. Asking permission wasn't working, either.

> **Resistance arose there, too. Asking permission wasn't working, either.**

The Aftermath

Out of cash and out of time, the founders decided to wind the company down in January 2018. The California legislation was eventually signed into law on September 18, 2018, legalizing the sale of home-cooked food, provided that individual California counties followed suit, because they would have to provide the necessary local oversight. But the cities and countries didn't like the new bill. One, the City of Chino Hills, argued that it would create "new and potential serious health risks to the public and create new enforcement challenges for our staff."

By September 2020, selling food cooked in home kitchens was legal in only one California county. Apparently, getting laws updated or changed is a complicated and lengthy process, with the future outcome and implementation highly uncertain. Asking permission, it seems, may well be unlikely to align with many entrepreneurs' aspirations and their timetables for getting there!

Lessons Learned About Not Asking Permission—and More

The practice of not asking permission and (perhaps) eventually begging forgiveness is a tricky and complicated issue, as we've seen. As Julie Samuels, the executive director of Tech:NYC, an advocacy organization for New York city's rapidly growing technology industry, observes on behalf of Tech:NYC's more than 300 member companies, "For a long time, the advice was, just keep your head down, build the kind of network you need to be viable, and then once you have viability, nobody is going to be able to shut you down."[41]

That's exactly what the TeamLease founders did, though with their heads held high, and their strategy panned out. As Sabharwal says, "We have built our business on the transmission losses between how the law is written, interpreted, practiced, and enforced. How it's written has not changed, but how it's interpreted, practiced and enforced is completely different."[42]

But taking that approach when there is legal ambiguity or when there is no applicable legislation at all is entirely different from doing so when what's **If what you plan to do is plainly illegal, my advice is to forget about your idea and move on.** being done is clearly illegal, as was the case with Josephine's home cooking. It's not difficult to examine up front which is the case in any particular situation. If there's regulatory ambiguity, as was the case for Uber and TeamLease, the Samuels advice may well apply. As Samuels also noted, "If Uber had gone to the regulators first, the entrenched interests would have crushed them in seconds."[43] But, when the law is clear, ignoring it is no excuse. If what you plan to do is plainly illegal, my advice is to forget about your idea and move on. So what are the lessons to take way from this chapter?

On taking the high road: Travis Kalanick's "principled confrontation" served Uber well in enabling it to reach scale unencumbered by regulatory issues. TeamLease, too, as they pursued the lofty ideal of "putting India to work." Arguing for lofty principles when your business plainly runs counter to existing regulations, however, is probably a fool's errand: a "rookie mistake" for Josephine's Jorgensen, perhaps, who had limited entrepreneurial experience prior to Josephine.

On getting laws changed: Jorgensen was probably naïve in believing that engaging with the regulatory authorities in Portland or elsewhere would bring about different results than had played out in Alameda County, and that any such changes could happen quickly. The wheels of justice almost always turn very slowly, and not just in India. Even when laws change, getting them implemented is a nontrivial matter. As we've seen, despite a 2018 change in the California law, selling home-cooked meals from one's kitchen remained a nonstarter in almost all of the state.

Part of the challenge, as Jorgensen discovered, is that the regulators only *enforce* the laws. It's politicians who *write* the laws. And opposition may arise from unexpected sources, as Jorgensen discovered, despite a well-intentioned entrepreneur's argument to the contrary. Even for Manish Sabharwal of TeamLease, who has made Herculean efforts toward labor reform in India, the left-leaning political parties have thwarted his efforts. Fortunately for TeamLease, as Sabharwal reports, "Just as I have not been able to get a *fatwa* issued to get the labor laws changed, the left parties have not been able to get a *fatwa* issued to shut me down."[44] The stalemate continues, while TeamLease thrives and more Indians get to work.

On public fights and visibility: If you are pursuing what you believe to be lofty ideals in which you fervently believe, it can be helpful, as we saw with Uber and TeamLease, to be forthright and public about those beliefs and ideals. Doing so may enable you to get your customer community to articulate similar views, which may, in turn, encourage regulators and lawmakers to take their constituents' views into account. When Uber was nearly shut down in London, the public outcry, supported by a 35,000-signature petition to Mayor Sadiq Khan to keep Uber operating, was no doubt helpful to Uber. For most politicians, voters' views matter at some level.

As Uber's Kalanick discovered, having a public fight over his company's right to operate played another role, too. It likely made consumers who had not yet ridden with Uber take note and give Uber a try. As they say in the public relations world, almost any publicity is good publicity, and most welcome, most of the time!

On the appropriateness (or not) of taking the law into your own hands: Bradley Tusk, a political consultant who worked with Uber to fight against restrictions proposed by then New York City Mayor Bill de Blasio, observes, "The fault, I think, is on both sides. On the tech side, I think sometimes we're arrogant. We always choose to beg for forgiveness rather than ask for permission and when we beg for forgiveness, we're not very nice about it. On the government side, they're doing the bidding of entrenched interests and campaign donors."[45]

So is it appropriate for entrepreneurs to set sail into uncharted waters where the law has not yet ruled or where the laws are in conflict with one another? That's a moral and ethical issue for which there's not always a clear answer. Sometimes, however, societies make progress when bold entrepreneurs take them forward. It's your call. Who would have invented the on-demand ride-hailing industry if not Camp and Kalanick? Who would have put India to work if a pair of plucky entrepreneurs hadn't done it? Who will make *your* corner of today's world a better place, if not *you*?

Bonus Lesson Learned

This chapter has delivered another set of lessons, to encourage you—where it's not clearly illegal to do so—to simply get on with your venture instead of asking permission. But there's another lesson here, too, about funding "get-big-fast" strategies and what to consider before doing so.

On the tension between pouring money into getting big fast and preserving your own ownership and

your freedom: Getting large enough that the regulators or other authorities won't shut you down, as both Uber and TeamLease did with considerable success, is often a matter of pursuing an abundance of venture capital with a goal of "getting big fast."

If you've got your own capital—or your employer's capital—with which to do that, as Sabharwal and Reddy did at TeamLease, so much the better. But taking boatloads of capital from investors, especially early on before your venture is proven, has some material downsides:

- **Raising capital is a full-time job.** Who will be minding the store and seeking to understand and serve customers if you're out raising capital? And a word to the wise: Once you've taken your first check, where will your attention likely turn? That's right, to the question of where your next check will come from in 12 to 18 months' time. Venture capital is a drug, and it's very difficult to get off it! Fund-raising is a huge distraction, and one that, once you set out on that path, never really goes away.

- **Raising capital from investors comes with baggage**—a shareholders' agreement. As one VC told me years ago, "The term sheet giveth; the shareholders' agreement taketh away." You may be pleased when you see your first term sheet, but I guarantee you won't like all the details to which you will likely have to eventually agree to get your hands on the investors' money!

- **Raising capital early means giving away a significant piece of your pie**, as compensation for the risk that every start-up entails. And your freedom, too, thanks to the shareholders' agreement. Manish Sabharwal offers some sage advice, "Bring on the best people as early as you can, and take outside money as late as you can."[46]

How to Add Never Asking Permission to *Your* Entrepreneurial Mindset

There are two sides of the coin we've examined in this chapter: skipping the permission up front and, if it becomes necessary, begging forgiveness later. But begging forgiveness may not turn out to be necessary at all, if what you are doing garners the support your venture needs—from consumers or clients, regulators, lawmakers, and more. The problem is that, as an aspiring entrepreneur entering a legally ambiguous venture that, like all new ventures, is laced with other uncertainties as well, you don't know up front how your journey will play out.

Thus, first, a modicum of humility, even contriteness, of the kind that Dara Khosrowshahi demonstrated after taking the reins at Uber, is probably in order. Travis Kalanick's no-holds-barred leadership style may have served Uber well in dealing with its regulators, but it surely did not do so with Uber's oft-harassed employees and its underappreciated drivers. And it cost Uber riders, too, because some consumers deleted Uber's app from their phones and switched to Lyft or other providers.

Second, your company's culture matters. Treat it with care. Don't confuse being tough in battling for your ideas in the marketplace, as both Uber and TeamLease did successfully, with what it takes to build a culture that works internally over the long term.

Third, do your homework. If you're about to enter a regulated industry, make sure you understand the legal framework that currently exists. You may find laws that conflict with one another or that are not consistently enforced, as was the case for TeamLease. You may find that the law is silent on the innovative approach or the new business model that you plan to pursue, as for Uber and the many start-ups whose business models rely on gig workers today. If so, skipping the permission and setting out boldly may be the best course of action. But if what you propose to do is clearly illegal under the current regulatory framework, as was the case for Josephine—and the founders knew it was illegal—I suggest you stop now.

Closing Thoughts

The principle of never asking permission doesn't just apply in legally or ethically ambiguous situations, though such situations bring the merits of this practice into sharp relief, as you've seen in this chapter. If you work where you have a boss, should you ask permission every step of the way? Not if you want to keep your job for very long! If you work with teammates, should you ask their permission for every step you need to take? Surely not. You're expected, in most managerial and entrepreneurial settings, to gather the best data you can, exercise good judgment, and make a sound decision about what to do next. In today's rapidly changing markets and industries, decision-making autonomy matters. Time won't wait!

❝If you work where you have a boss, should you ask permission every step of the way?❞

As Manish Sabharwal puts it, "If you wait for all the lights to be green, you'll never leave home."[47] Every new venture is faced with an abundance of uncertainty. If you are an aspiring entrepreneur setting out on a new venture or someone trying to grow one that's already underway, or even a big-company leader trying to coax your people into thinking more counter-conventionally, embrace the uncertainty. Mitigate the risks however you can (more on that topic in the next and final chapter). And treat your venture as the bundle of hypotheses that it really is, each of which awaits affirmation or rejection. I suggest that, most of the time, you can skip the permissions and simply muster up the courage to get on with your journey, as so many successful entrepreneurs have done before you. Give it a go!

8

Act Your Way to a New Way of Thinking (Because the Reverse Won't Work!): From Mindsets to Action

Instead of asking permission, beg forgiveness later

Yes, we can!

Your counter-conventional mindset

Beg, borrow, (but don't steal)

Problem-first, not product-first logic

Ask for the cash, ride the float

Think narrow, not broad

Why was it that it took Jeff Bezos, instead of someone working in a large bookstore chain such as Borders or Barnes & Noble, to create an online bookstore, and then the Kindle, and then so much more? Why was it Elon Musk—instead of someone at Ford, Renault, or Toyota—who put the necessary oomph (and capital!) behind electric vehicles to suddenly make them relevant? Why did it take two industry outsiders like Garrett Camp and Travis Kalanick to connect the dots, create the gig-worker phenomenon, and reinvent the taxi industry? Why did it take two Indian entrepreneurs, Manish Sabharwal and Ashok Reddy—instead of the well-endowed multinational temporary staffing firms—to jump-start the temporary help industry in India and put millions of Indians to work? Was it their break-the-rules mindsets, perhaps? Or, more pertinently, in the industry you want to enter or where you work today, why not *you*?

In this closing chapter, it's my goal to set you on your way toward adopting one or two—or even more, if you're someone like Chapter 1's Lynda Weinman—of the six entrepreneurial mindsets that I've revealed in this book. To do so, I'll first address your likely starting point, which will vary from reader to reader, and then point out the formidable obstacles you're likely to face, and how to overcome them. If I'm lucky—no, if you're plucky!—you've already begun the process, using the lessons you've found at the end of each chapter. In reality, though, many of you will have wanted to finish reading the book and absorbing the inspiring and compelling case studies herein, before heading down that counter-conventional path. Well, now's the time to get started!

What You Should Do Now Depends on Your Starting Point

There are several likely audiences reading this book. Some of you are aspiring entrepreneurs, just getting started on the exciting and potentially career-altering or life-changing task of identifying an opportunity that will deliver on your entrepreneurial dreams. Some are already well along the entrepreneurial path, no doubt, looking to find product-market fit, perhaps, or looking to grow your business now that fit's been achieved. Others work for or perhaps lead much larger businesses, whether fast-growing "gazelles" or slower growing corporates, as did Nespresso's Éric Favre and Jean-Paul Gaillard. You may well see yourselves as potential catalysts or spark plugs for jump-starting your company's next growth spurt, by taking advantage of an opportunity you've identified that holds considerable potential.

And, perhaps surprising to the aforementioned groups, some of you may be students, whether undergraduates or more seasoned graduate students, with an eye toward becoming or

> **Wouldn't you rather be the master or mistress of your own destiny or work for a fast-growing company that creates abundant opportunities for personal growth for its people?**

working for an entrepreneur in the future, whether sooner or later. After all, wouldn't you rather be the master or mistress of your own destiny or work for a fast-growing company that creates abundant opportunities for personal growth for its people? If you are such a student, perhaps your teacher or professor has assigned this book as a pragmatic, real-world resource, as so many have done with my earlier trade books. Let's take each of these groups in turn.

Aspiring Entrepreneurs

Of particular use to you will be Chapter 3 (problem-first, not product-first logic) and Chapter 4 (think narrow, not broad) and the real-world lessons you've already discovered in the final sections thereof. Once these chapters have led you to an opportunity that fits your mission, your aspirations, your risk propensity, and your skills and capabilities, Chapter 5 will help you finance it with your customer's cash. If Elon Musk can ask his first customers to slap down $100,000 for a new Tesla Roadster before he'd even built one, you can ask for cash up front, too! Yes, it takes courage. But fear not and ask!

Those Already Traveling the Entrepreneurial Path

You've already identified your target customer, perhaps, or perhaps not. Or you've got a first-generation product or prototype coming out of the lab, an MVP, as Eric Reis calls it.[1] Or not. Or you're growing fast with your initial offering (as Phil Knight finally was with Nike, some five years down the line), and ready to build on what you've learned and launch something new (Nike's tennis and basketball shoes came next).

A great starting point for you is Chapter 3 (problem-first, not product-first logic) to get you out of your product-first mindset and into problem-solving mode. Chapter 5 (ask for the cash, ride the float) and Chapter 6 (beg, borrow, but don't steal) will help you, too, to finance either those early steps or your next spurt of growth. If your customers are asking you for something you've not done before, Chapter 2 (Yes, we can!) will give you the courage, perhaps, to step out of your comfort zone and find a way to give them what they're asking for.

Anyone Else in Business Elsewhere

Every business these days wants its people to be more entrepreneurial, it seems. Rarely, however, do their leaders know exactly what they mean. Do they want more out-of-the-box thinking? Probably. Be more counter-conventional? Perhaps, if the right leadership is in place. More innovation? For sure. Do they want more risk? Not so much! Saying "Yes, we can!" (Chapter 2) is likely to be an uphill slog in your situation, as Tom Peters's and C. K. Prahalad's advice that your company stick to its knitting and build on its core competencies may be principles that are firmly held in your company. Failing to ask permission (Chapter 7) probably won't endear you to the company lawyers or leaders, either.

A key question you might want to ask yourself, in whatever business and in whatever line of work you're in, is whether your boss wants you to stick your neck out and act independently. It depends on the company culture, as well as your boss' management style, I suppose. Where your company's culture permits, and where your boss welcomes your initiative, the break-the-rules mindsets revealed in Chapters 3 through 6 are eminently deployable in almost any organization of any size, in any industry. You can get your start at thinking and acting more counter-conventionally, more entrepreneurially, with any of them.

Or, just maybe, *you* are the leader and you've been charged with or taken on the daunting task of getting your slow-growing company out of its rut. What you probably need is get a few brave people onto your bus, as Jim Collins puts it, to start breaking some of the conventional rules! I suggest you give them this book, or at least Chapters 3 through 6, and let them get on with it!

What If You're a Student?

These days, a substantial portion of the MBA students who enroll where I teach at London Business School do so with the explicit goal of becoming entrepreneurs. Find an idea. Find a co-founder. Raise some money, and let's go! That's also true at many other institutions of all kinds, graduate and undergraduate.

If you are among these highly motivated students intent on making your own way in the world, you've come to the right place. This book has equipped you with a toolkit of six counter-conventional, break-the-rules mindsets, and there's little point in waiting to put them to good use. As you're probably in the "aspiring" camp I mentioned earlier, I suggest you follow my advice there. Some of you may already be further along the path—I see start-ups founded by surprisingly young people all the time—in which case any of Chapters 2 through 7 are a good place to start.

And for All of You

All those reading this book have their own distinct personalities. Some of the six mindsets will be more easily and more comfortably adopted by some of you than by others. At this point in the book, you'll already have an idea of which of the six mindsets fit who *you* are. But, I caution you, getting out of our comfort zones is how we all grow, as human beings and as businesspeople. So don't let your lack of comfort stand in your way.

You might want to talk about the six mindsets with like-minded friends and colleagues, even your spouse or boss, if you have one. You can reread a chapter or two to make sure you've got their lessons down pat, but what I really hope you'll do is act. Now. Identify an important problem to solve. Borrow the assets you need. Ask for your customers' cash. And get *your* entrepreneurial ball rolling. There's much that needs changing in this world we live in today, and there are few who are better equipped to drive those changes than entrepreneurs like you, wherever you live, wherever you work.

So What's to Stop You?

❝Putting the mindsets revealed in this book into action in your life and your business isn't going to happen by just *thinking* differently.❞

Best-selling authors Richard Pascale, Jerry Sternin, and Monique Sternin said it all in their 2010 book, *The Power of Positive Deviance*. "You cannot think your way into a new way of acting, you have to act your way into a new way of thinking."[2] So putting the mindsets revealed in this book into action in your life and your business isn't going to happen by just *thinking* differently. It isn't going to happen easily, either, for there are four formidable obstacles that stand in your way.

To firmly embed the lessons you can take from this book and set you on a path toward making at least a couple of the six mindsets your own, it's important that we examine these four key obstacles and see what can be done about them. Unfortunately, each of them has the power to stop you in your tracks and prevent you from using these mindsets to connect what you encounter or observe in your world—whatever your starting point—with the necessary actions to enable you to attain the aspirations you hold. Without sustained effort on your part—acting, not just thinking—and without a healthy dose of experimentation, these obstacles will surely defeat you! Here they are:

- Risk: Why big companies don't like it and how to manage or mitigate it
- Faulty assumptions: How to challenge them
- Analysis paralysis: How to overcome it
- The dark side of entrepreneurship: How to confront it

Obstacle 1: Risk, and How to Manage or Mitigate It

Let's face facts. Most big companies don't like risk. As the former Sun Microsystems co-founder and now venture capital investor Bill Joy wrote back in 2004, "Big companies almost never innovate. This is unfortunate because innovation is one of the few ways to gain proprietary advantage and stay profitable."[3] Sadly, Joy's words still ring true today.

With innovation comes risk. Why don't big companies like risk, when innovation is so central to their future success? In my experience, risk calls to the forefront the possibility of failure. Big companies, especially those traded on public stock exchanges, are asked to deliver consistent quarter-after-quarter results to their shareholders. Almost by definition, big new ideas, whether new products or new ventures, with their high risk of failure that I noted in Chapter 1, simply don't fit. Why change something that seems to be working just fine? So let's dig a bit deeper into the risk aversion issue and why it's so salient today.

In business schools like mine, risk and its attendant challenges are top of mind. My finance colleagues, for example, provide our students with a variety of tools to keep risk at bay.[4] They teach our students and executives to seek risk-adjusted returns so that riskier projects are asked to deliver superior returns, compared to those for low-risk projects. They provide tools so that future cash flows are "discounted" at rates that vary according to the anticipated level of risk. The greater the risk of future returns, the less is the "present value" at which they're to be counted at the present time.[5] My strategy colleagues ask for a section or a chapter in every strategic plan that outlines the attendant risks.[6] Our behavioural economists study how people treat downside losses differently from upside gains and how we can avoid the hidden biases that are likely to be the result.[7] Risk is on everyone's agenda, it seems. Might *your* counter-conventional mindset hold the key to combatting all this preoccupation with risk?

If you're working in a big company today, you probably are witnessing such risk aversion first-hand. Perhaps your company's innovation effort has been outsourced to an M&A team. "Open innovation," it's euphemistically called. Don't bother to invent; acquire.[8] Perhaps your company's "innovation" effort has been delegated to a small innovation unit for which budgets are modest (so that the inevitable failures don't move the corporate needle too far downward) and big successes are rare. But at least you're allowed to experiment with new ideas. Or, worse, perhaps your new ideas simply fall on deaf ears when the capital allocation committee meets.

Will one or more of the mindsets in this book provide you with a path forward? You've probably already seen in the "Lessons" sections of Chapters 2 through 7 that, indeed, one or more of them will do just that, depending on the form of the current obstacles your company puts in your way.

Thus, a key role the mindsets revealed in this book play is to help entrepreneurs and other innovators mitigate or manage the attendant risk. They beg, borrow (and, sadly, sometimes steal) resources, to avoid putting money at risk. They ask for up-front cash from their customers to avoid taking on investors or lenders—or going to the corporate treasurer—with the risk and loss of control that doing so might entail. They think narrowly about their target market and use problem-first logic to enhance their customer understanding and thereby enhance their chances of achieving product-market fit, so that customers buy. And so on.

> **Thus, a key role the mindsets revealed in this book play is to help entrepreneurs and other innovators mitigate or manage the attendant risk.**

Thus, most entrepreneurs I know don't lose much sleep over risk. Jeff Bezos selected a leader, Steve Kessel, who assembled a two-pizza team to get started on creating the Kindle. Sunil Bharti Mittal, having reached critical mass in the Indian mobile phone industry in 2003, saw that rural markets were the next frontier. By offloading onto his key suppliers (hence "borrowing") the assets that would be necessary to sustain profitable growth therein, he, too, mitigated risk. I'd argue that both are among the Jedi Masters of the risk-mitigation craft.

Thus, contrary to the folklore, entrepreneurs don't much like risk either. They use these six mindsets to mitigate it. Or manage it. Or off-load it onto others. "Isn't your idea risky?" they will be asked. Of course, it's risky! There's market risk: Will customers buy (They bought from the outset at Budgetplaces. com; but not so fast at Nespresso.)? There's technology risk: Will the new-fangled product actually work (Would Elon Musk figure out how to build electric vehicles with enough range?)? There's execution risk: Will the team be able to deliver what it sets out to deliver (Simon Cohen's 2 a.m. wake-ups stole a day on his competitors.)? And more. Working counter-conventionally, they all put one or more of the six mindsets into action. You can, too!

Obstacle 2: Faulty Assumptions, and How to Challenge Them

These days, assumptions are littered nearly everywhere on the entrepreneurial or new product landscape, it seems. Every spreadsheet is built upon nothing more than a series of assumptions, line after line, cell by cell. The phrase, "We *believe* that . . . blah, blah blah," appears in nearly every business plan I read. What it usually means is "We *fervently hope and pray* that . . . blah, blah, blah." There's only one effective way to challenge assumptions, really. And challenge them you must, for many of them will, inevitably, turn out to be erroneous. That one way is by gathering evidence. Hard, cold facts. So what if you were to treat every assumption you encounter— or as Randy Komisar and I call them, leaps of faith—as something to be tested as an hypothesis instead? [9]

In my experience, a proposed new idea or new venture of any kind—whether one conceived in a college entrepreneurship class, in a co-working space, at your kitchen table or in your

> **"Thus, risk reduction and experimentation—in order to challenge your or others' untested assumptions—are inextricably intertwined."**

garage, or deep inside a large company that hopes to grow faster—is, at the outset, little more than a bundle of hypotheses that will either be affirmed or rejected as the early days of new venture unfold. As at least some of those hypotheses are—hopefully!—affirmed with what I hope will be low-cost and fast experiments, one after another, risk is reduced. Thus, risk reduction and experimentation—in order to challenge your or others' untested assumptions—are inextricably intertwined.

You can challenge assumptions and reduce risk—at least by a little bit—by researching the market, for example. But what prospective customers *say* they will do is not necessarily what they will *actually do* when it's time to pull out their wallets. So mere market analysis will not suffice if you want to materially reduce risk (and you do!). Alberto Savoia's wonderful 2019 book, *The Right It*, offers numerous simple, practical, and effective tools for gathering what he calls YODA—Your Own DAta—so you can avoid what he calls the Law of Market Failure that the overwhelming majority of new ideas will fail soon after launch.[10] Combining Savoia's methods while employing problem-first logic (Chapter 3) and focusing on a very narrow target market (Chapter 4) is your way forward.

Saying, "Yes, we can!" (Chapter 2) is an assumption, too, of course, at least until you've figured out how to deliver whatever you've just promised. Asking for the customer's cash up front (Chapter 5) is an assumption that's only affirmed once you receive payment (and the check clears!). "Borrowing" the assets you'll need to get started and until demand is proven (Chapter 6) is an assumption until the deal is secured. Even skipping permission is an assumption as well, until you make enough progress to learn that your gamble was a good one (for Josephine, it wasn't, as we saw in Chapter 7).

A key question every entrepreneur of every shape and kind must ask is "Why *won't* my idea work?"[11] Experiments to challenge your and others' untested assumptions—about product demand, about the viability of your business model, and more, are your way forward. If you're unable to overturn your early assumptions, and unable to prove them faulty, you may well be on to something special!

Obstacle 3: Analysis Paralysis, How to Move Beyond Thinking, and Act

It is widely known that entrepreneurs tend to have an inherent bias for action and for learning by doing. "Analysis paralysis" is not a disease with which most of the successful ones have been afflicted. "Ready, fire, aim," is more like it. They try something and see whether it works. Experimentation, of course, amounts to just that.

When you say "Yes, we can!" to a customer who requests something you've not done before, you'll then have to figure out just how you're going to deliver, as we saw SubWay Link's Arnold Correia do in Chapter 2. For entrepreneurs, though, figuring that out means acting, not merely thinking. Correia didn't sit and ponder where he might find someone who could shoot a video of that event. He got on his cell phone and asked around. When he needed satellite capacity for Corporate TV, he quickly used his network to find someone with spare capacity he could "borrow."

When Garrett Camp and Travis Kalanick conceived Uber, as we saw in Chapter 7, they didn't think very much about whether it was legal to get started. They simply got started. TeamLease's Manish Sabharwal and Ashok Reddy did ask that question, of course. When they discovered the legal ambiguity that was evident in India's unruly thicket of labor laws, they pounced, putting India to work, while the large multinational temporary staffing firms already present in India, though at very modest levels, held back. Bias for action, indeed! You can adopt such a bias, too! As I've suggested earlier, "Just do it!"

Obstacle 4: The Dark Side, and How to Confront It

Entrepreneurs are admired by many, but not always revered. Sometimes they are castigated; sometimes despised. In particular, begging forgiveness instead of asking permission, as we saw in

"Entrepreneurs are admired by many, but not always revered. Sometimes they are castigated; sometimes despised. "

Chapter 7, sometimes walks a very fine line between what is legal and ethical and what's not. Your reputation matters, so be careful what you do with it! But there's more to watch out for.

Elon Musk's tendency to run roughshod over those who disagree with him does not endear him to many, despite his legion of fawning fans. The black cab drivers with whom I ride in London are fans of neither Travis Kalanick nor Uber. Labor union leaders in India belittle the temporary employment that TeamLease has delivered to so many who were previously unemployed or marginally employed, even though nearly all of them, once hired, have remained employed for the long term. Independent booksellers where Amazon does business don't appreciate Amazon's having pulled their often meager but typically impassioned living out from under many of them, as their shops have suffered or closed.

Thus, developing the mindsets you've learned herein might present downsides, along with the upsides the case studies in this book have revealed. Buyer beware! If you believe in your cause, however, that you are resolving an important set of customer problems—or even delivering customer delight, as Starbucks arguably does, at least most of the time—you might be well served to consciously weigh the trade-offs you might face.

The good news is this. Much of the progress that our societies make is driven by entrepreneurs like Manish Sabharwal and Ashok Reddy of TeamLease in addressing India's employment problem, Elon Musk's efforts toward climate change, and the connectivity and other benefits that Sunil Bharti Mittal and other telecom pioneers have brought to rural India and Africa. We don't want to lose that progress! Go forth and change the world or at least your small part of it. That's what we entrepreneurs do best! Who knows, the next Elon Musk or Manish Sabharwal just might be you!

Closing Thoughts

To be sure, entrepreneurs' bias for action and for learning by doing sets them apart from many other individuals. But not all of us are naturally wired that way. I know very few entrepreneurs who regularly put anything like all six of these mindsets to work. Linda Weinman, whom you met in Chapter 1, is an exception. In fact, as I studied some of today's most accomplished entrepreneurs and the extent to which they apply these mindsets, I found something surprising. In a sample of 138 accomplished entrepreneurs running fast-growing, successful businesses, the mean number of the six mindsets that they reported as characterizing the way they work was 3.4.[12] Few in that sample exhibited all six!

What this means to me is that you don't have to adopt or master all six counter-conventional mindsets today or tomorrow. It may be that one of them fits a situation in which you find yourself today. Another might fit what you encounter tomorrow. But, your temperament willing, and with a willingness to act, you can learn to apply some of them to break the conventional rules, for sure. Today *and* tomorrow! So, get on with your journey! I wish you *Bon voyage*!

Notes

Preface: Why This Book?

1. Bill Joy, "Large Problem: How Big Companies Can Innovate," *Fortune*, November 15, 2004, p. 214.

Chapter 1: It's Time to Break the Rules: Challenge Assumptions, Overcome Obstacles, Mitigate Risk

1. Except where otherwise noted, the Lynda Weinman case study is sourced from Jane Porter, "Hit the Ground Running: From Near Failure to A $1.5 Billion Sale: The Epic Story of Lynda.com," *Fast Company*, April 27, 2015, https://www.fastcompany.com/3045404/from-near-failure-to-a-15-billion-sale-the-epic-story-of-lyndacom; and Guy Raz and Liz Metzger, "How I Built This, Lynda.com: Lynda Weinman and Bruce Heavin," NPR podcast, September 6, 2021, https://www.npr.org/2021/09/03/1034004284/lynda-com-lynda-weinman-and-bruce-heavin.
2. Raz and Metzger, "How I Built This."
3. Porter, "Hit the Ground Running."
4. Raz and Metzger, "How I Built This."
5. Tiffany Pham, "How She Did It: Lynda Weinman, from Web Graphics and Design to Cofounder of Lynda.com," *Forbes*, January 20, 2015, https://www.forbes.com/sites/tiffanypham/2015/01/20/lynda-weinman-from-renowned-web-graphics-and-design-expert-to-co-founder-of-lynda-com.
6. Raz and Metzger, "How I Built This."
7. Porter, "Hit the Ground Running."
8. Raz and Metzger, "How I Built This."
9. Ibid.
10. Ibid.

11. Ibid.
12. Ibid.
13. Rachel Emma Silverman and Nikki Waller, "Lynda.com: A 60-Year-Old Earns Internet Glory," *Wall Street Journal*, April 9, 2015, https://www.wsj.com/articles/lynda-com-a-60-year-old-earns-internet-glory-1428625176.
14. Ibid.
15. Raz and Metzger, "How I Built This."
16. Carol S. Dweck, *Mindset: The New Psychology of Success* (New York, Random House, 2007).
17. http://sourcesofinsight.com/what-is-mindset/.
18. Vinod Khosla, "Any Big Problem Is a Big Opportunity," eCorner, https://ecorner.stanford.edu/videos/any-big-problem-is-a-big-opportunity/, accessed June 28, 2022.
19. Francesca Gino, *Rebel Talent: Why It Pays to Break the Rules at Work and in Life* (New York: Dey Street/William Morrow, 2018), p. xiii.
20. Margaret Mead, quoted at https://www.brainyquote.com/quotes/margaret_mead_100502, accessed June 28, 2022.

Chapter 2: When You're Tempted to Say No, Instead Say "Yes, We Can!": Then Figure Out How

1. Tom Peters and Robert Waterman, *In Search of Excellence: Lessons from America's Best-Run Companies* (New York: Harper Business, 1982).
2. C. K. Prahalad and Gary Hamel, "The Core Competence of the Corporation," *Harvard Business Review* 68, no. 3 (1990): 79–91.
3. "The Breakup of GE and J&J: The End of the Conglomerate?" *Knowledge at Wharton*, November 16, 2021, https://knowledge.wharton.upenn.edu/article/the-breakup-of-ge-and-jj-the-end-of-the-conglomerate/?utm_source=kw_newsletter&utm_medium=email&utm_campaign=2021-11-16.
4. John Mullins and Randy Komisar, *Getting to Plan B* (Boston: Harvard Business Press, 2009).
5. Casey Newton, "The Everything Book: Reading in the Age of Amazon," *The Verge*, December 17, 2014, https://www.theverge.com/2014/12/17/7396525/amazon-kindle-design-lab-audible-hachette.

6. This section is largely sourced from Colin Bryar and Bill Carr, *Working Backwards: Insights, Stories, and Secrets from Inside Amazon* (New York: St. Martin's Press, 2021); and Brad Stone, *The Everything Store* (New York: Little, Brown, 2013).

7. Bryar and Carr, *Working Backwards*, p. 162.

8. Jane Black, "Where 'Think Different' Is Taking Apple," *BusinessWeek Online*, August 5, 2003, http://www.businessweek.com/technology/content/aug2003/tc2003085_3215_tc112.htm. Retrieved from the Factiva Database.

9. Bryar and Carr, *Working Backwards*, p. 168.

10. Stone, *The Everything Store*, p. 234.

11. For more on Amazon's core leadership principles, see Bryar and Carr, *Working Backwards*, pp. 14–16.

12. Ibid., p. 14.

13. Ibid., p. 180.

14. Ibid., p. 182.

15. Stone, *The Everything Store*, p. 237.

16. Ibid., p. 238.

17. Ibid., p. 239.

18. Ibid., p. 247.

19. Ibid., p. 245.

20. Rick Munarriz, "Oprah Saves Amazon," *Motley Fool*, October 27, 2008, https://www.fool.com/investing/general/2008/10/27/oprah-saves-amazon.aspx.

21. Stone, *The Everything Store*, p. 255.

22. Ibid., p. 253.

23. Newton, "The Everything Book."

24. The information in this section is sourced largely from Alessandro Ananias, Brian Forde, and John Mullins, "SubWay Link (A)" and "SubWay Link (B)," London Business School, 2013.

25. Ananias, Forde, and Mullins, "SubWay Link (A)," p. 3.

26. Ibid., p. 4.

27. Ibid., p 5.

28. Ananias, Forde, and Mullins, "SubWay Link (B)," p. 2.

29. Ibid., p. 4.

30. This section is largely sourced from Tiffany Putimahtama and John Mullins, "MOVE Guides (A)," "MOVE Guides (B)," and "MOVE Guides (C)," London Business School, 2019.

31. Abbie Griffin and Albert L. Page, "An Interim Report on Measuring Product Development Success and Failure," *Journal of Product Innovation Management* 10, no. 4 (September 1993): 291–308.

32. Putimahtama and Mullins, "MOVE Guides (B)," p. 2.

33. Ibid., p. 4.

34. Ibid., p. 5.

35. Ibid.

36. Putimahtama and Mullins, "MOVE Guides (C)," p. 1.

37. Ibid., p. 3.

38. Ibid., p. 4.

39. Ibid.

40. Ibid., p. 5.

41. For a useful framework for rigorously assessing opportunities, see John Mullins, *The New Business Road Test*, 5th ed. (London: FT Publishing, 2017).

42. For more on business models and how to assess them, see John Mullins and Randy Komisar, *Getting to Plan B* (Boston: Harvard Business Press, 2009).

43. For more on Amazon's "Bar Raiser" hiring practices, see Bryar and Carr, *Working Backwards*, pp. 34–51.

44. https://dictionary.cambridge.org/us/dictionary/english/acquihire.

45. For more on Amazon's two-pizza teams, see Bryar and Carr, *Working Backwards*, pp. 65–67.

46. For more on how to get customers—rather than investors—to fund your business, see John Mullins, *The Customer-Funded Business* (Hoboken, NJ: Wiley, 2014).

47. Jim Collins, *Good to Great* (New York: Harper Business, 2001), Chapter 3.

48. Recommended by John Hall, "7 Books to Help You Improve Your Business Networking and Build Real Relationships," *Forbes*, December 17, 2017, https://www.forbes.com/sites/johnhall/2017/12/17/7-books-to-help-you-improve-your-business-networking-and-build-real-relationships/?sh=303887dd68ae.

Chapter 3: It's the Customer's Problem That Matters, Not Your Solution: Problem-First, Not Product-First, Logic

1. Bill Joy, "Large Problem: How Big Companies Can Innovate," *Fortune*, November 15, 2004.

2. John W. Mullins and Orville C. Walker, Jr., *Marketing Management* (New York: McGraw-Hill, 2013), p. 261.

3. Vinod Khosla, "Any Big Problem Is a Big Opportunity," eCorner, Stanford University, accessed December 8, 2020 at https://ecorner.stanford.edu/videos/any-big-problem-is-a-big-opportunity/.

4. The material in this section, except where otherwise noted, was sourced from Phil Knight, *Shoe Dog* (New York: Scribner, 2016); and John Mullins, *The New Business Road Test* (Harlow, UK: Pearson, 2018), Chapter 2.

5. Knight, *Shoe Dog*, p. 9.

6. Ibid., p. 48.

7. Ibid., p. 80.

8. Ibid., p. 195.

9. Ibid., p. 197.

10. Ibid.

11. The material in this section was sourced from Darice Gubbins, John Walker, and John Mullins, "Simon Cohen (A)," London Business School, 2011.

12. Ibid., p. 2.

13. Ibid., p. 5.

14. Ibid.

15. Ibid., p. 6.

16. Ibid., p. 7.

17. Ibid., p. 10.

18. The material in this section, except where otherwise noted, was sourced from John Mullins, "Silverglide Surgical Technologies (A)" and "Silverglide Surgical Technologies (B)," London Business School, 2004.

19. Personal conversation with the author, August 2021.

20. Mullins, "Silverglide Surgical Technologies (A)," p. 4.

21. Ibid.

22. Ibid., p. 5.

23. Khosla, "Any Big Problem."

24. Mullins, "Silverglide Surgical Technologies (B)," p. 2.

25. SilverGlide® Bipolar Non-Stick Forceps, Stryker Neuro Spine ENT, 2009, p. 4. Accessed September 3, 2021 at https://www.stryker.com/content/dam/stryker/navigation/products/silverglide/resourcesk/SilverGlide-Bipolar-Forceps-brochure.pdf.

26. The material in this section, except where otherwise noted, was sourced from David Prinster and John Mullins, "Apex Ski Boots (A)" and "Apex Ski Boots (B)," London Business School, 2018.

27. Prinster and Mullins, "Apex Ski Boots (A)," p. 2.

28. Ibid., p. 3.

29. Prinster and Mullins, "Apex Ski Boots (B)," p. 2.

30. Ibid.

31. Ibid.

32. Ibid.

33. https://www.apexskiboots.com/, accessed September 3, 2021.

34. Ibid.

35. Personal conversation with the author, August 2021.

36. For the PayPal story, see John Mullins and Randy Komisar, *Getting to Plan B: Breaking Through to a Better Business Model* (Boston: Harvard Business Press, 2009), p. 4.

37. For more on the idea of going the extra mile in business, see Amar Bhidé's classic article, "Hustle as Strategy," *Harvard Business Review*, September–October 1986.

38. For more on organizational culture and how to build a strong one, see Edgar Schein's iceberg model in Edgar H. Schein, *Organizational Culture and Leadership* (San Francisco: Jossey-Bass, 1992). For more on how and why Simon Cohen built his company's culture, see Simon Cohen, *Fulfilled*, independently published, 2021.

39. To learn more about assessing entrepreneurial opportunities more fully, see John Mullins, *The New Business Road Test: What Entrepreneurs and Investors Should Do Before Launching a Lean Start-Up*, 5th ed. (London: FT Publishing, 2018).

Chapter 4: Why "Moving the Needle" Doesn't Matter Much to Entrepreneurs: Think Narrow, Not Broad

1. For more on the stage-gate process, see Robert G. Cooper, "Selecting Winning New Product Projects: Using the NewProd System," *Journal of Product Innovation Management* 2, no. 1 (March 1985): 34–44; and R. G. Cooper, "Next Stage for Stage-Gate," *Pragmatic Marketer* (Winter 2014): 20–24.

2. "Critical Pitfalls of the NPD Process," Hanover Research, October 31, 2016, https://www.hanoverresearch.com/reports-and-briefs/new-product-development-process-pitfalls/.

3. House of Switzerland, "Éric Favre—The Swiss Inventor Who Put Coffee into Capsules," June 7, 2017, https://houseofswitzerland.org/swissstories/economics/eric-favre-swiss-inventor-who-put-coffee-capsules.

4. Ed Cumming, "How Nespresso's Coffee Revolution Got Ground Down," *The Guardian*, July 14, 2020, https://www.theguardian.com/food/2020/jul/14/nespresso-coffee-capsule-pods-branding-clooney-Nestlé-recycling-environment.

5. Liz Alderman, "Nespresso and Rivals Vie for Dominance in Coffee War," *New York Times*, August 20, 2010, https://www.nytimes.com/2010/08/21/business/global/21coffee.html?searchResultPosition=4.

6. Joyce Miller and Kamran Kashani, "Innovation and Renovation: The Nespresso Story," IMD, 2000, p. 9.

7. Ibid.

8. Ibid., p. 12.

9. Cumming, "How Nespresso's Coffee Revolution Got Ground Down."

10. Carol Matlack, "Nespresso Pitches 'Luxury' Coffee for Lean Times," Bloomberg.com, March 24, 2009, https://www.bloomberg.com/news/articles/2009-03-24/nespresso-pitches-luxury-coffee-for-lean-times.

11. Jean-Paul Gaillard, LinkedIn, accessed January 20, 2022.

12. The material for this section, except where otherwise indicated, was sourced from Chavie Lieber, "The Charmed Life of Pandora," Racked.com, August 23, 2016, https://www.racked.com/2016/8/23/12525316/pandora-jewelry-charm-bracelets; Coleby Nicholson, "Birth of Brand Pandora," *Jeweller Magazine*, June 1, 2008, https://www.jewellermagazine.com/Article.aspx?id=234; Natalia Rachlin, "A Danish Fairy Tale Gone Awry," *New York Times*, December 6, 2011, https://www.nytimes.com/2011/12/07/fashion/07iht-ACAJ-PANDORA07.html; interviews with Martin Hoyer-Hansen and Nikolaj Velsgaard, March 16 and 17, 2015; and Elizabeth Philp and John Mullins, "Pandora (A)" and "Pandora (B)," London Business School, August 2017.

13. Philp and Mullins, "Pandora (A)," p. 1.

14. Ibid, p. 2.

15. Ibid., pp. 2–3.

16. Ibid., p. 3.

17. Ibid.

18. Lieber, "The Charmed Life of Pandora."

19. Philp and Mullins, "Pandora (A)," p. 3.

20. Ibid., pp. 5–6.

21. Philp and Mullins, "Pandora (B)," p. 2.

22. Ibid.

23. Ibid., p 4.

24. Rachlin, "A Danish Fairy Tale."

25. Margot Patrick, "Denmark's Pandora Jumps in Debut," *Wall Street Journal*, October 5, 2010, https://www.wsj.com/articles/SB10001424052 7487037264045755333241795470962.

26. Rachlin, "A Danish Fairy Tale."

27. The material in this section was sourced, except where otherwise noted, from Hicham Sharara and John Mullins, "Visual Optical (A)" and "Visual Optical (B)," London Business School, 2006.

28. Sharara and Mullins, "Visual Optical (A)," p. 6.

29. Ibid., p. 7.

30. Ibid., p. 8.

31. Ibid.

32. Sharara and Mullins, "Visual Optical (B)," p. 3.

33. Ibid.

34. Author interview with Aziz Mebarek and Karim Trad, October 7, 2005.

35. Ibid.

36. To learn about disciplined ways of getting to something that will actually work, see Alberto Savoia, *The Right It* (New York: Harper One, 2019); and John Mullins and Randy Komisar, *Getting to Plan B* (Boston: Harvard Business Press, 2009).

37. For more on how to build an entrepreneurial team around the critical success factors required in your industry, see John Mullins, *The New Business Road Test*, 5th ed. (London: FT Publishing, 2017), Chapter 7.

38. For a structured approach to thinking about the economics of your business model, see Mullins and Komisar, *Getting to Plan B*.

39. Cited in House of Switzerland, "Éric Favre."

40. For a more complete treatment of market segmentation and targeting, see John W. Mullins and Orville Walker, Jr., *Marketing Management* (New York: McGraw-Hill, 2013), Chapter 7.

41. For more on designing and carrying out marketing research, see Mullins and Walker, Jr., *Marketing Management*, Chapter 6; and Mullins, *New Business Road Test*, Chapters 11 and 15.

Chapter 5: How Entrepreneurs Get Things Done with Almost No Money: Ask for the Cash, Ride the Float

1. Jerry Useem, "The Stock-Buyback Swindle," *The Atlantic*, August 2019, https://www.theatlantic.com/magazine/archive/2019/08/the-stock-buyback-swindle/592774/.

2. Ibid.

3. For a discussion of the drawbacks of this kind of VC-driven thinking, see John Mullins, *The Customer-Funded Business* (Hoboken, NJ: Wiley, 2014), Chapter 1.

4. For the story of the genesis of Michael Dell's Dell Computing, see his autobiography, *Direct from Dell* (New York: Harper Business, 1999).

5. Dana Hull and Hannah Recht, "Tesla Doesn't Burn Fuel, It Burns Cash," Bloomberg.com, April 30, 2018, https://www.bloomberg.com/graphics/2018-tesla-burns-cash/.

6. CrunchBase, "Tesla," https://www.crunchbase.com/organization/tesla-motors/company_financials, accessed February 9, 2022.

7. Ashlee Vance, *Elon Musk: Tesla, SpaceX, and the Quest for a Fantastic Future* (New York: Harper Collins, 2015), p. 163.

8. Tim Higgins, *Power Play: Tesla, Elon Musk, and the Bet of the Century* (New York: Doubleday, 2021), p. 49.

9. Christopher McFadden, "The Short But Fascinating History of Tesla," Interesting Engineering, https://interestingengineering.com/the-short-but-fascinating-history-of-tesla, accessed February 4, 2022.

10. Higgins, *Power Play*, p. 93.

11. Ibid., p. 112.

12. Vance, *Elon Musk*, p. 288.

13. Ibid., p. 289.

14. Ibid.

15. Higgins, *Power Play*, p. 165.

16. Fred Lambert, "Tesla Has Over 24,000 Model X Reservations, Twice as Much as They Had for the Model S," *Electrek*, June 30, 2015, https://electrek.co/2015/06/30/tesla-has-over-24000-model-x-reservations-twice-as-much-as-they-had-for-the-model-s/.

17. Tim Higgins, "Tesla Asks Suppliers for Cash Back to Turn a Profit," *Wall Street Journal*, July 22, 2018, https://www.wsj.com/articles/tesla-asks-suppliers-for-cash-back-to-help-turn-a-profit-1532301091.

18. Michael J. Coren, "Tesla Keeps Finding Ways to Keep Wall Street Happy and Cash in the Bank," Quartz.com, July 31, 2018, https://qz.com/1334234/tesla-keeps-gaming-the-system-to-turn-a-profit/.

19. Lora Kolodny, "Tesla Is Asking Model 3 Reservation Holders for Another $2500 to Order Their Cars," CNBC.com, June 28, 2018, https://www.cnbc.com/2018/06/28/tesla-model-3-orders-cost-2500-more.html.

20. Hull and Recht, "Tesla Doesn't Burn Fuel."

21. The material in this section was sourced from Shira Conradi and John Mullins, "Budgetplaces.com (A)" and "Budgetplaces.com (B)," London Business School, 2014.

22. Conradi and Mullins, "Budgetplaces.com (A)," p. 3.

23. Ibid.

24. Ibid., p. 7.

25. Ibid.

26. Ibid., p. 9.

27. Ibid.

28. "John Erceg, Founder and CEO, Budgetplaces.com," video, London Business School, 2015.

29. The material in this section is sourced from Ambika Patni, Shreedhar Munshi, and John Mullins, "The Loot (A)" and "The Loot (B)," London Business School, 2013.

30. Patni, Munshi, and Mullins, "The Loot (A)," p. 2.

31. Ibid., p. 5.

32. Ibid., p. 6.

33. Ibid., p. 7.

34. Ibid.

35. Ibid., p. 8.

36. For the remarkable story of how Airbnb got its start, see Mullins, *Customer-Funded Business.*

37. For more on minimum viable products, see Steve Blank, *The Four Steps to the Epiphany: Successful Strategies for Products That Win* (Hoboken, NJ: Wiley, 2020).

38. To learn more about the five different models for securing customer funding, see Mullins, *Customer-Funded Business.*

39. Hull and Recht, "Tesla Doesn't Burn Fuel."

40. Ibid.

41. Author conversation with Jon Smith, Pobble founder and CEO, September 17, 2021.

42. Carol S. Dweck, *Mindset: The New Psychology of Success* (New York: Random House, 2007).

Chapter 6: Make the Future Winnings Yours!: Beg, Borrow, But Don't Steal

1. For an extensive treatment of how to methodically go about getting from Plan A to Plan B, see John Mullins and Randy Komisar, *Getting to Plan B* (Boston: Harvard Business School Publishing, 2009).

2. Except as otherwise noted, this section was sourced from "Bharti Airtel Ltd. history, profile and corporate video," https://www.companieshistory.com/bharti-airtel/, accessed December 1, 2021; *Knowledge at Wharton*, "Bharti Group's Sunil Bharti Mittal on Lessons of Entrepreneurship and Leadership," https://knowledge.wharton.upenn.edu/article/bharti-groups-sunil-bharti-mittal-on-lessons-of-entrepreneurship-and-leadership/, July 10, 2008; and "History of Bharti Tele-Ventures Limited," https://www.referenceforbusiness.com/history2/12/Bharti-Tele-Ventures-Limited.html, accessed December 1, 2021.

3. *Knowledge at Wharton*, "Bharti Group's Sunil Bharti Mittal."

4. Ibid.

5. Henny Sender, "Bharti's Stock Price May Not Show Potential—Issues Plunge Despite Prospects for Growth," *Wall Street Journal Europe*, April 30, 2002.

6. *Knowledge at Wharton*, "Bharti Group's Sunil Bharti Mittal."

7. Rebecca Buckman, "Outsourcing with a Twist: Indian Phone Giant Bharti Sends Jobs to Western Firms in Multinational Role Switch," *Wall Street Journal*, January 18, 2005.

8. F. Asis Martinez-Herez and V.G Narayanan, *Strategic Outsourcing at Bharti: One Year Later* (Harvard Business School Publishing, 2006), p 3.

9. "India Telecommunication: The Growth Continues," Morgan Stanley Equity Research, March 6, 2006.

10. "Bharti AirTel, Ltd. (BHARTI-ARTL) – Company History," https://www.business-standard.com/company/bharti-airtel-15542/information/company-history.

11. Ibid.

12. The Luxy Hair case history is sourced from Benjamin Hallen and John Mullins, "Big Beautiful Hair," London Business School, 2019.

13. "Alex and Mimi Ikonn, Luxy Hair Co-Founders video," London Business School, March 2016.

14. Ibid.

15. Author conversations with Mimi and Alex Ikonn, July 2015.

16. Ibid.

17. The GoApe case history is sourced primarily from Stephanie Hussels and David Molian, "GoApe! Live Life Adventurously Case Study Part A: Monkeying Around," *International Review of Entrepreneurship* 8, no. 4 (2020): 337–346; Stephanie Hussels and David Molian, "GoApe! Live Life Adventurously Case Study Part B: Eight Hundred Pound Gorilla," *International Review of Entrepreneurship* 8, no. 4 (2020): 347–356; and numerous conversations among Tristram and Rebecca Mayhew and the author between 2013 and 2022.

18. Hussels and Molian, "GoApe!," p. 340.

19. Ibid., p. 342.

20. Conversation with the author, May 2014.

21. Ibid.

22. John Mullins, "Go Ape (C)," London Business School, March 2017, pp. 2–3.

23. Kendall Taggart, "A Data Team Tied to Trump's Campaign Has a Pretty Unusual Past," *BuzzFeed*, January 21, 2017, https://www.buzzfeednews.com/article/kendalltaggart/company-tied-to-trump-campaign-once-pushed-voter-suppression.

24. Matthew Rosenberg, Nicholas Confessore, and Carole Cadwalladr, "Firm That Assisted Trump Exploited Data of Millions," *New York Times*, March 18, 2018, https://www.nytimes.com/2018/03/17/us/politics/cambridge-analytica-trump-campaign.html.

25. John Koetsier, "This Big Data Marketing Firm Claims to Have a Perfect Track Record in Winning Elections," Forbes.com, November 9, 2017, https://www.forbes.com/sites/johnkoetsier/2017/11/09/trumps-election-data-firm-has-100-track-record-in-winning-elections/?sh=2632ee6a5c91.

26. Rosenberg, Confessore, and Cadwalladr, "Firm That Assisted Trump."

27. Sam Meredith, "Facebook-Cambridge Analytica: A Timeline of the Data Hijacking Scandal," CNBC.com, April 10, 2018, https://www.cnbc.com/2018/04/10/facebook-cambridge-analytica-a-timeline-of-the-data-hijacking-scandal.html.

28. Federal Trade Commission, "FTC Imposes $5 Billion Penalty and Sweeping New Privacy Restrictions on Facebook," July 24, 2019, https://www.ftc.gov/news-events/news/press-releases/2019/07/ftc-imposes-5-billion-penalty-sweeping-new-privacy-restrictions-facebook.

29. Paola Zialcita, "Facebook Pays $643,000 Fine for Role in Cambridge Analytica Scandal," NPR.org, October 30, 2019, https://www.npr.org/2019/10/30/774749376/facebook-pays-643-000-fine-for-role-in-cambridge-analytica-scandal#:~:text=In%20its%20investigation%2C%20the%20ICO,people%20without%20their%20consent%20worldwide.

30. Olivia Solon and Oliver Laughland, "Cambridge Analytica Closing after Facebook Data Harvesting Scandal," *The Guardian*, May 2, 2018, https://www.theguardian.com/uk-news/2018/may/02/cambridge-analytica-closing-down-after-facebook-row-reports-say.

31. For a detailed discussion of the five customer-funded models, see John Mullins, *The Customer-Funded Business* (Hoboken, NJ: Wiley, 2014).

32. Reid Hoffman, *Masters of Scale*, https://mailchi.mp/mastersofscale/strategy-session?e=0989f08086, accessed June 23, 2022.

33. For more on the benefits of a sense of belonging among your workforce, see Susie Lee, "Why Belonging Is Key to Building the New Workforce," *MIT Sloan Management Review*, June 13, 2022, https://sloanreview.mit.edu/article/why-belonging-is-key-to-building-the-new-workforce/.

34. Bruce Golden, interviewed by author on "How to Finance and Grow Your Startup—Without VC," https://www.coursera.org/learn/startup-financing-without-vc.

Chapter 7: What Entrepreneurs Can Do That Big Companies Can't: Instead of Asking Permission, Beg Forgiveness Later

1. Thomas Donaldson, "Values in Tension: Ethics Away from Home," *Harvard Business Review*, September–October 1996.

2. Except where otherwise noted, this section was sourced from Kara Swisher, "Man and Uber Man," *Vanity Fair*, December 2014, https://www.vanityfair.com/news/2014/12/uber-travis-kalanick-controversy; Mike Isaac, "Uber Suspends Operations in a Deal with City Regulators," *New York Times*, December 18, 2014, https://bits.blogs.nytimes.com/2014/12/18/uber-suspends-portland-operations-in-deal-with-city-regulators/; Todd C. Frankel and Elizabeth Dwoskin, "Why Travis Kalanick Didn't Survive at Uber," *Washington Post*, June 21, 2017, https://www.washingtonpost.com/business/economy/why-travis-kalanick-didnt-survive-uber/2017/06/21/8ecb98d6-51d3-11e7-be25-3a519335381c_story.html; and Alanna Petroff, "London Says It Won't Renew Uber's License," *CNN Business*, September 22, 2017, https://money.cnn.com/2017/09/22/technology/uber-london-license/index.html?iid=EL.

3. Swisher, "Man and Uber Man."

4. Ibid.

5. Ibid.

6. Ibid.

7. Ibid.

8. Isaac, "Uber Suspends Operations."

9. Frankel and Dwoskin, "Why Travis Kalanick."

10. Travis Kalanick, "A Profound Apology," *Uber Newsroom*, March 1, 2017, https://www.uber.com/newsroom/a-profound-apology.

11. Frankel and Dwoskin, "Why Travis Kalanick."

12. Petroff, "London Says It Won't Renew."

13. Mansoor Iqbal, "Uber Revenue and Usage Statistics (2022)," Business of Apps.com, February 17, 2022, https://www.businessofapps.com/data/uber-statistics/.

14. This section is sourced from Payne Miller, Qusai Kanchwalla, and John Mullins, "Concept Arbitrage in India (A)" and "Concept Arbitrage in India (B)," London Business School, 2011.

15. Miller, Kanchwalla, and Mullins, "Concept Arbitrage in India (A)," p. 2.

16. Ibid., p. 4.

17. Ibid., p. 8.

18. Ibid., p. 9.

19. Ibid., p. 10.

20. Manish Sabharwal, in "Manish Sabharwal" video, London Business School, 2016.

21. Miller, Kanchwalla, and Mullins, "Concept Arbitrage in India (B)," p. 3.

22. Sabharwal, "Manish Sabharwal" video.

23. Ibid.

24. Author conversation with Ashok Reddy, April 27, 2011.

25. Ibid.

26. Ibid.

27. Sabharwal, "Manish Sabharwal" video.

28. Author conversation with Manish Sabharwal, March 25, 2021.

29. Except where otherwise noted, this section is sourced from Katelan Cunningham, "Startup Stories: How Josephine Is Building Community for Home-Cooked Takeout," *ThinkApps*, January 26, 2015, http://thinkapps.com/blog/launch/startup-stories-josephine-building-community/; Leilani Clark, "Josephine Wants to Bring the Sharing Economy to Your Kitchen," *Civil Eats*, August 10, 2015, https://civileats.com/2015/08/10/josephine-com-wants-to-bring-the-sharing-economy-to-your-kitchen/; Kate Williams, "Food Startup Josephine Pauses East Bay Operations," May 11, 2016, https://www.berkeleyside.org/2016/05/11/food-startup-josephine-pauses-east-bay-operations; Sarah Kessler, "The Food-Sharing Economy Is Delicious and Illegal—Will It Survive?" *Fast Company*, July 7, 2016, https://www.fastcompany.com/3061498/the-food-sharing-economy-is-delicious-and-illegal-will-it-survive?utm_source=postup&utm_medium=email&utm_campaign=gigged&position=5&partner=newsletter&campaign_date=08302021; and Megan Rose Dickey, "Food-Sharing Startup Josephine Doesn't Want to Be Like the Rest of the Sharing Economy," *TechCrunch*, August 16, 2016, https://techcrunch.com/2016/08/16/josephine-cook-equity/.

30. Kessler, "The Food-Sharing Economy."
31. Molly Turner, "Cooks First or Rules First? Josephine.com's Regulatory Struggles in the Shared Economy," Haas School of Business, University of California–Berkeley, August 1, 2019, https://www.scribd.com/document/506906892/Josephine-Case, p. 5.
32. Ibid., p. 7.
33. Ibid.
34. Ibid., p. 8.
35. Ibid., p. 9.
36. Ibid.
37. Kessler, "The Food-Sharing Economy."
38. Ibid.
39. Ibid.
40. Dickey, "Food-Sharing Startup Josephine."
41. Kessler, "The Food-Sharing Economy."
42. Sabharwal, "Manish Sabharwal" video.
43. Kessler, "The Food-Sharing Economy."
44. Sabharwal, "Manish Sabharwal" video.
45. Kessler, "The Food-Sharing Economy."
46. Author conversation with Manish Sabharwal, March 25, 2021.
47. Sabharwal, "Manish Sabharwal" video.

Chapter 8: Act Your Way to a New Way of Thinking (Because the Reverse Won't Work!): From Mindsets to Action

1. A minimum viable product. See Eric Reis, *The Lean Startup* (New York: Crown Business, 2011).
2. Richard Pascale, Jerry Sternin, and Monique Sternin, *The Power of Positive Deviance: How Unlikely Innovators Solve the World's Toughest Problems* (Boston: Harvard Business Review Press, 2010).
3. Bill Joy, "Large Problem: How Big Companies Can Innovate," *Fortune*, November 15, 2004, p. 214.
4. Richard Brealey, Stewart Myers, and Franklin Allen, *Principles of Corporate Finance* (New York: McGraw-Hill Education, 2019).
5. Ibid.

6. Vaughan Evans, *The FT Essential Guide to Writing a Business Plan* (London: FT Publishing, 2015); and Richard Rumelt, *Good Strategy/Bad Strategy* (London: Profile, 2017).

7. Richard Kahneman, *Thinking, Fast and Slow* (New York: Farrar, Straus and Giroux, 2011).

8. Henry Chesbrough, *Open Innovation* (Boston: Harvard Business School Press, 2003).

9. John Mullins and Randy Komisar, *Getting to Plan B* (Boston: Harvard Business Press, 2009).

10. Alberto Savoia, *The Right It* (New York: Harper One, 2019).

11. For a comprehensive treatment of how to address this key question, see John Mullins, *The New Business Road Test*, 5th ed. (London: FT Publishing, 2017).

12. The question I asked, after describing each of the six mindsets, was "To what extent has your career path been marked by this mindset?" The average response of 3.4 was the number of mindsets to which they replied 4 or 5 on a five-point scale, where 5 means "highly or regularly descriptive of my career path" and 1 means "rarely or not at all descriptive of my career path."

About the Author

John Mullins is a veteran of three start-ups and an award-winning professor and scholar at London Business School. He has been studying how businesses start, grow, and prosper for three decades. He has authored more than 50 case studies and has published more than 50 articles in a variety of outlets, including *Harvard Business Review*, the *MIT Sloan Management Review*, and the *Wall Street Journal*.

John's first book, *The New Business Road Test: What Entrepreneurs and Executives Should Do Before Launching a Lean Start-Up*, has become the definitive work on the assessment and shaping of entrepreneurial opportunities and is widely used by investors and entrepreneurs and in university courses worldwide.

His second book, the critically acclaimed *Getting to Plan B: Breaking Through to a Better Business Model*, co-authored with Randy Komisar, a partner at venture capital firm Kleiner Perkins, was named to "Best Books of the Year" lists by *BusinessWeek* and *Inc.* magazine.

John's third book, *The Customer-Funded Business: Start, Finance or Grow Your Company with Your Customers' Cash*, was named one of five not-to-be-missed books by *Fortune* magazine. It challenges the commonly held assumption that among an entrepreneur's first and most important tasks is that of raising investment capital. Its material provides the foundation for John's widely viewed online course on Coursera.com.

You can reach John directly on LinkedIn or at jmullins@ london.edu or learn more about him at www.johnwmullins .com. If any portion of this book resonates with the journey you have taken, John would love to hear from you!

When he's not on the road—or sometimes online, these days—delivering workshops for communities of entrepreneurs and other innovators, John can be found in London or hiking or skiing not far from Golden, Colorado, with his wife, Donna, and his daughters, Kristina and Heather.

Index